"LIBERTY ENLIGHTENING THE WORLD,"

BY BARTHOLDI.

(To be erected on Bedloe's Island, in the harbor.)

New York City in the 19th Century:

A Dramatic Collection of Images

By Mark Bussler

www.ClassicGameRoom.com

BROOKLYN BRIDGE. FRANKFORT STREET HEALY BUILDING.

NEW-YORK CITY.

LOOKING SOUTHEAST FROM THE "WORLD" DOME.

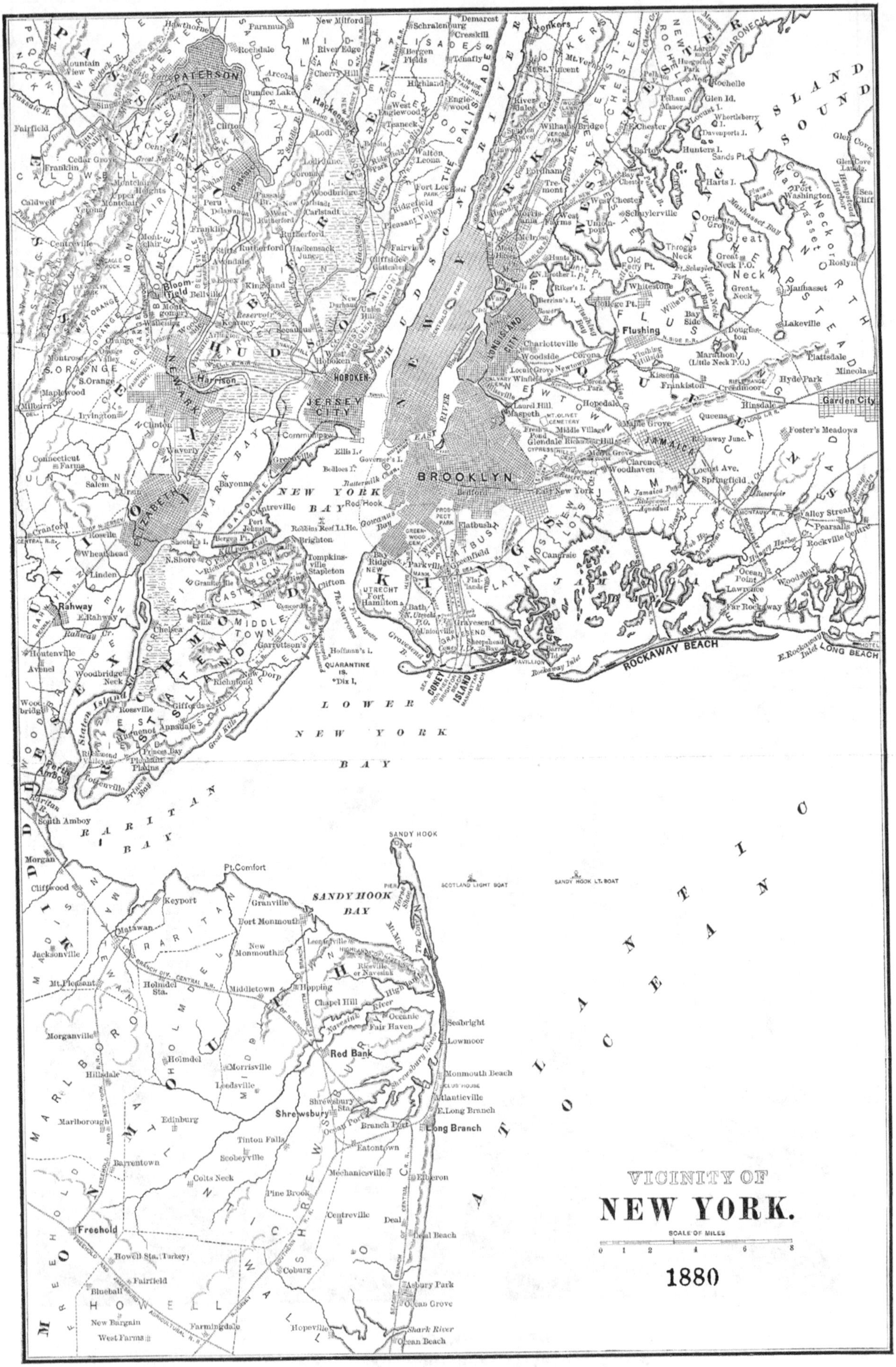
VICINITY OF
NEW YORK.
SCALE OF MILES
0 1 2 4 6 8
1880
PATERSON
NEWARK
JERSEY CITY
HOBOKEN
BROOKLYN
ELIZABETH
LONG ISLAND CITY
JAMAICA
Flushing
Yonkers
Hackensack
Harrison
Rahway
Perth Amboy
South Amboy
Red Bank
Shrewsbury
Long Branch
Freehold
Garden City
NEW YORK BAY
LOWER NEW YORK BAY
RARITAN BAY
SANDY HOOK BAY
SANDY HOOK
LONG ISLAND SOUND
ROCKAWAY BEACH
LONG BEACH
CONEY ISLAND
EAST RIVER
HUDSON RIVER
ATLANTIC OCEAN
SCOTLAND LIGHT BOAT
SANDY HOOK LT. BOAT
QUARANTINE IS.

New York from the Hudson.

New York from Fort Wadsworth, Staten Island.

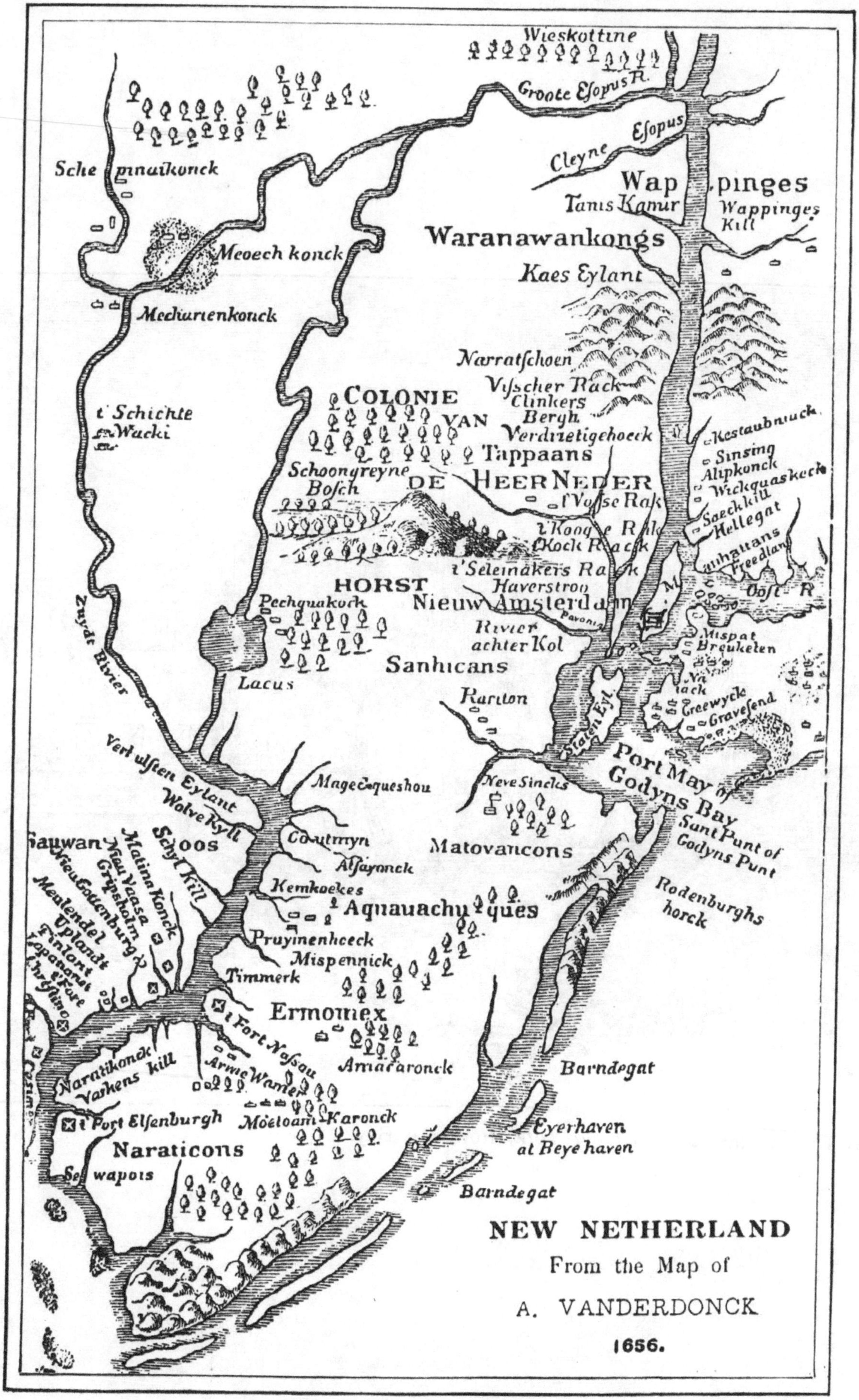

DUTCH MAP OF NEW YORK, 1656.

Lower Part of the City of New York, from the Bay.

View of New York from Brooklyn Heights.

Park Avenue.

Wall Street, with Treasury Building at the right, and Trinity Church at the head of the Street.

Broad Street, from corner of Wall Street.

Nassau Street north from Wall Street.

Upper part of Nassau Street.

Pine Street

The Approach to the East River Bridge.

Union Square.

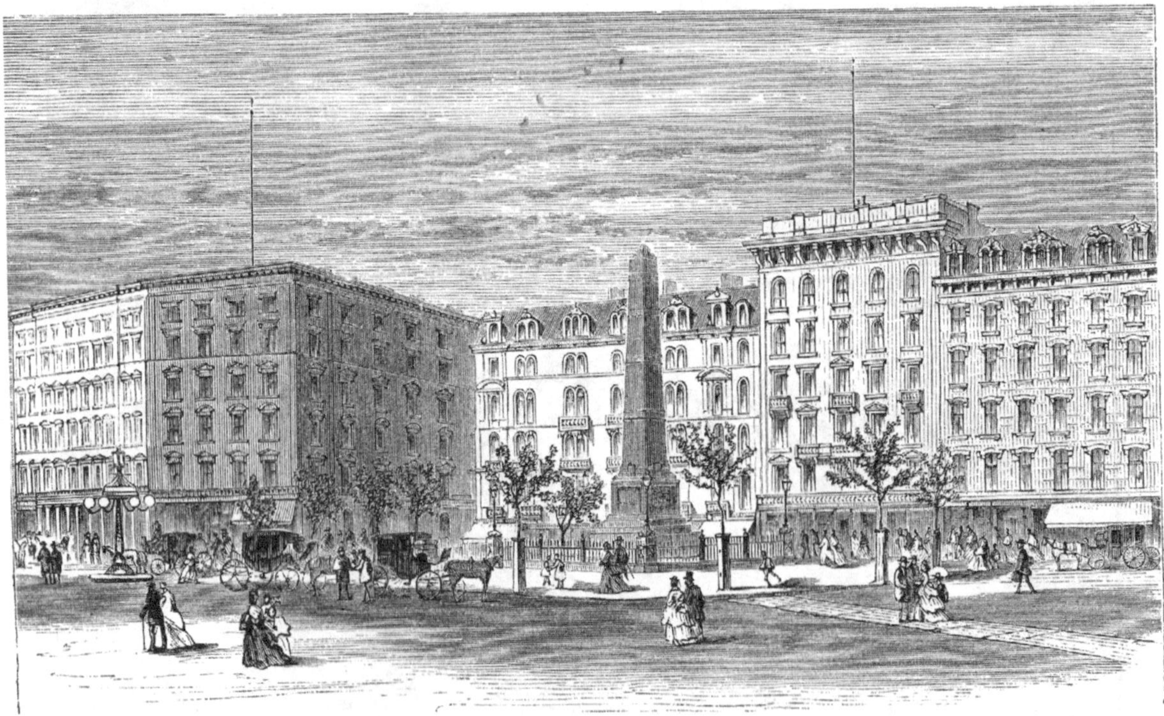

Broadway, West Side of Madison Square.

"The Victoria," Twenty-seventh Street.

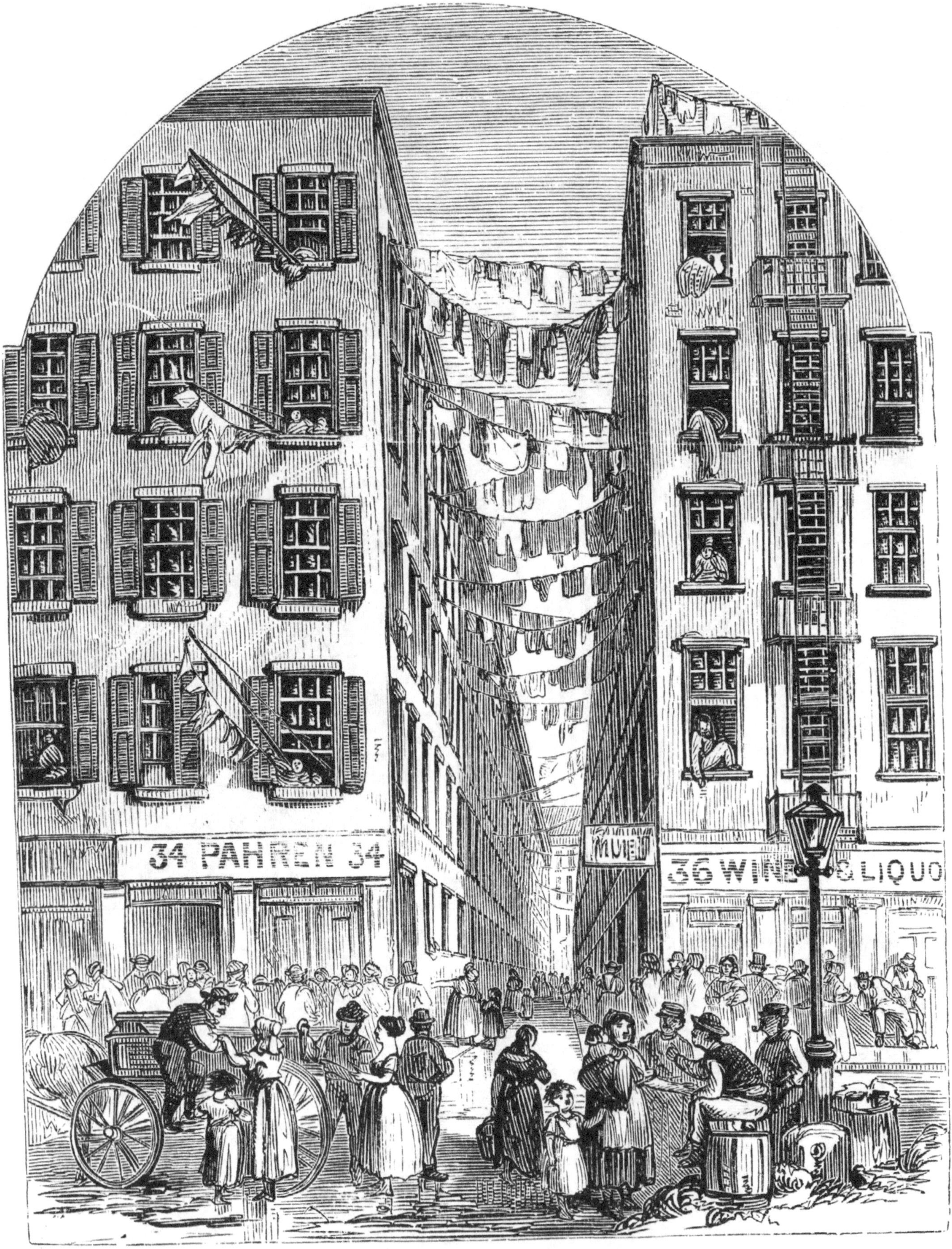

Tenement-Houses.

Twenty-third Street from corner of Fourth Avenue.

(Young Men's Christian Association Building on the left; National Academy of Design on the right.)

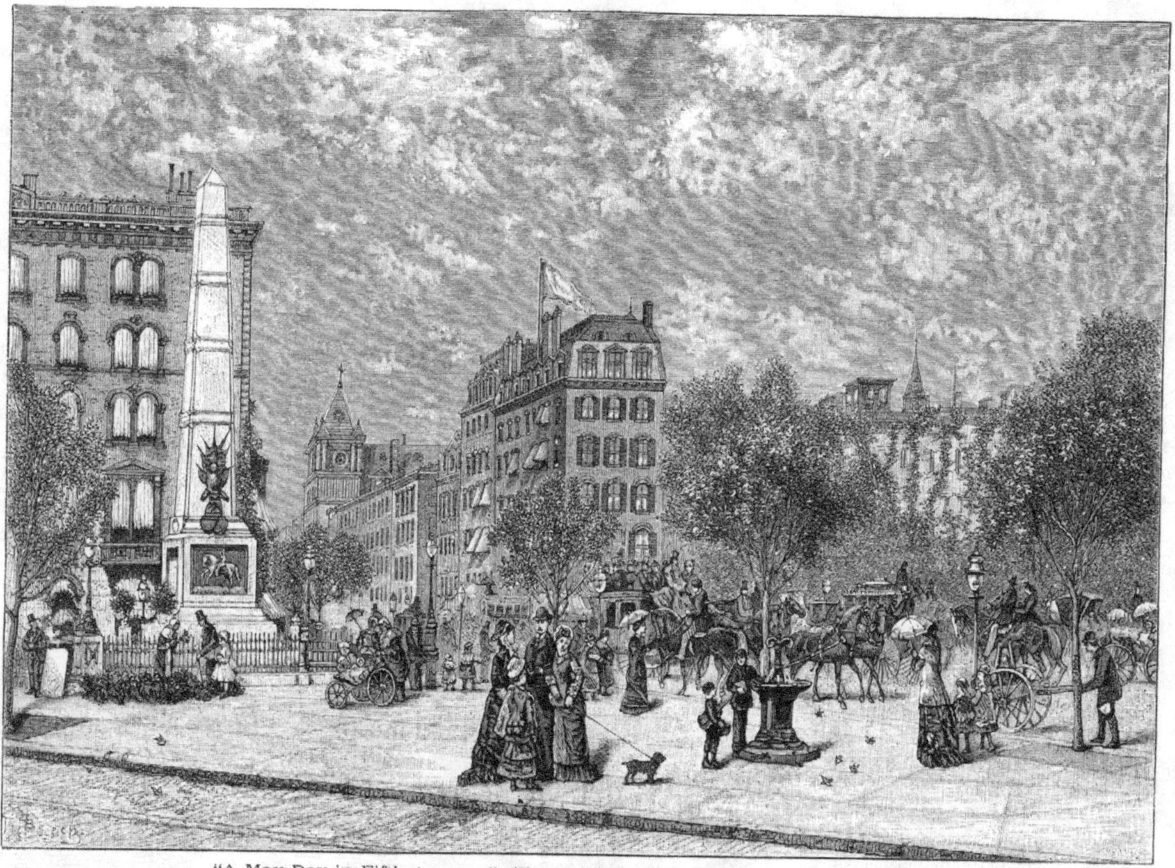

"A May-Day in Fifth Avenue" (From a Painting by Wordsworth Thompson.)

Market-Wagons Stand.

NEW YORK
BRISTOL
LIVERPOOL

South Street, below Burling Slip.

Fifth Avenue Scenes.

Fifth Avenue, at corner of Twenty-first Street.

Thirty-fourth Street, corner of Fifth Avenue.

Coaching Day.—Scene in Fifth Avenue.

Fifth Avenue - The Vanderbilt Mansions

Fifth Avenue and Fifty-sixth Street

The West Side Elevated Railroad at 110th Street.

Elevated Railway in Third Avenue

Corner of Sixth Avenue and Twenty-third Street, showing Elevated Railway and Station.

West Street, near Canal Street.

City Hall and New Court-House.

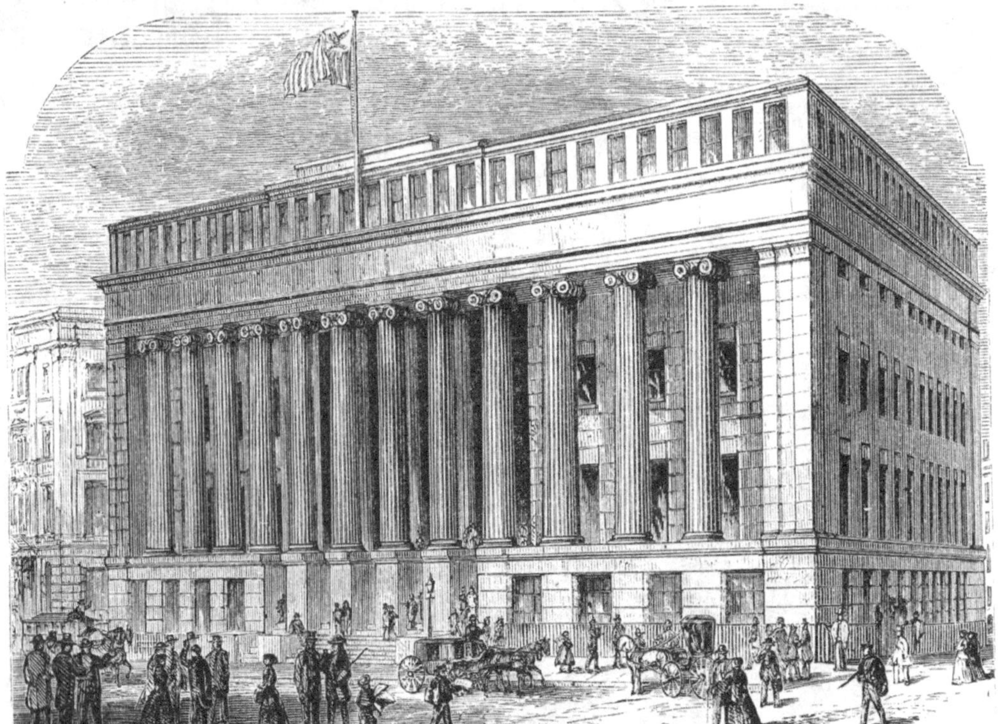

Custom-House, Wall Street.

Court-House, Sixth Avenue and Tenth Street.

Post Office, and U. S. Court Building.

City Prison, or " The Tombs.

Interior, Post-Office.

Columbia College. (New building.)

Astor Library, Lafayette Place.

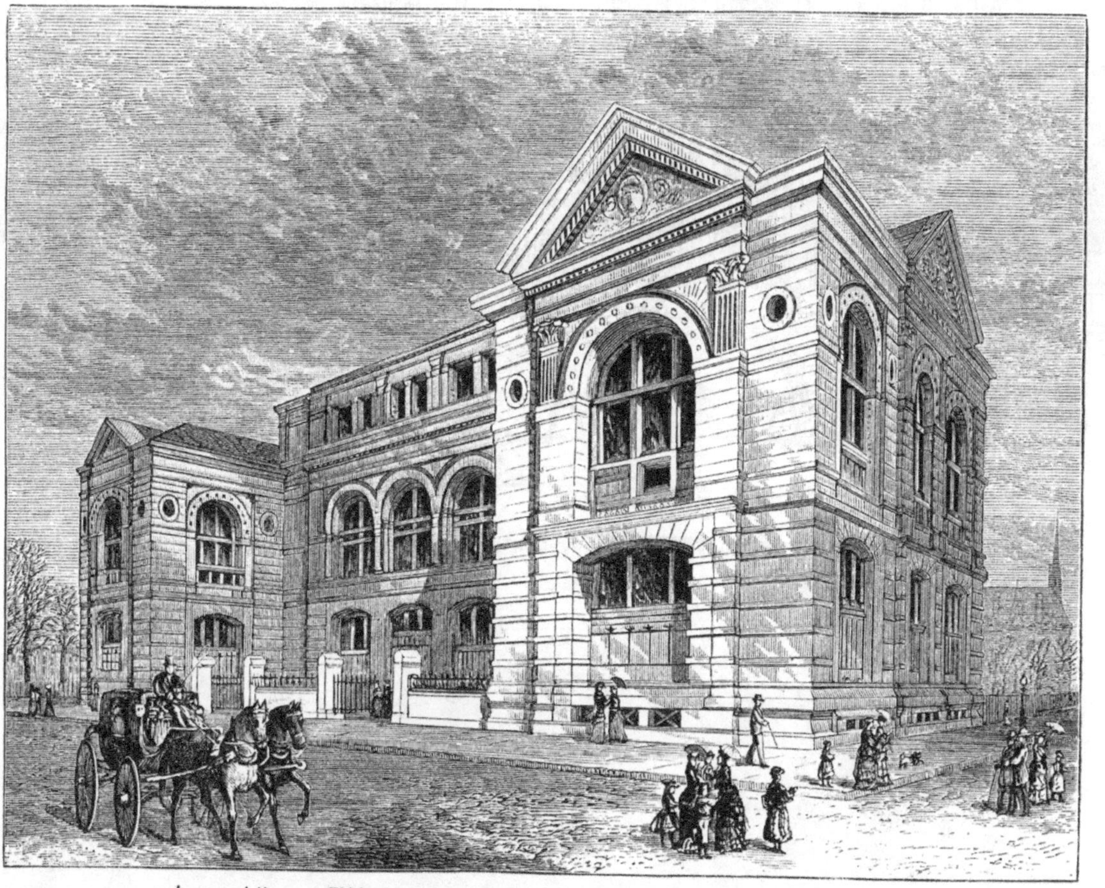

Lenox Library, Fifth Avenue, between Seventieth and Seventy-first Streets.

Normal College, Sixty-ninth Street.

St. Joseph's Home, Lafayette Place.

A Misty Morning.

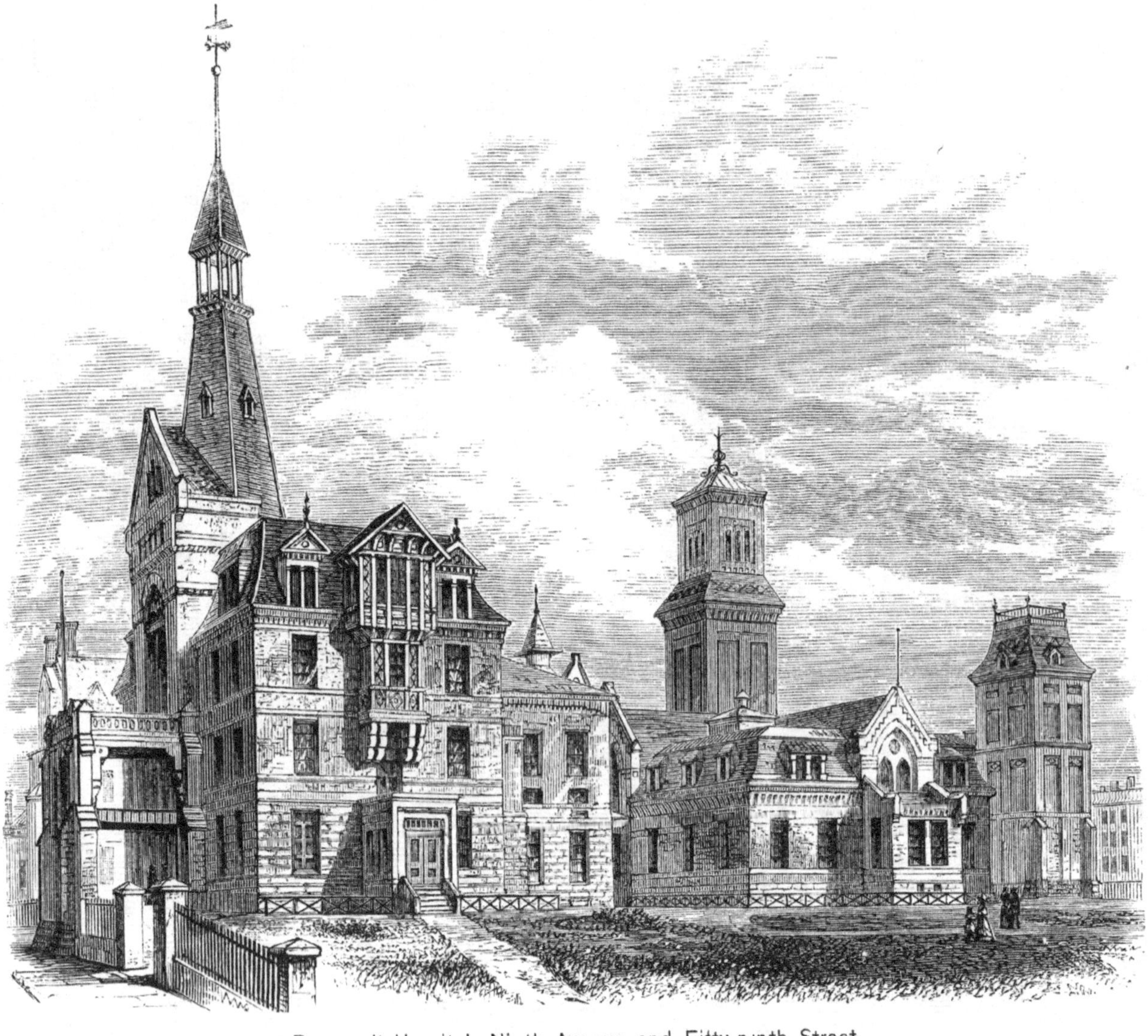

Roosevelt Hospital, Ninth Avenue and Fifty-ninth Street

The Presbyterian Hcspital, Seventieth Street.

Harlem Bridge.

Mount Sinai Hospital Sixty-sixth Street.

Masonic Temple, on Twenty-third Street and Sixth Avenue.

Booth's Theatre, corner of Twenty-third Street and Sixth Avenue.

Seventh Regiment Armory.

Union League Club, Fifth Avenue, corner Thirty-ninth Street.

The Grand Opera-House, corner of Twenty-third Street and Eighth Avenue.

"The Florence," East Eighteenth Street.

Park Avenue Hotel, Park Avenue and Thirty-third Street.

Western Union Company's Telegraph-Building, Broadway, corner Dey Street.

The "Tribune" and "Times" Buildings, Printing-House Square.

New York Life-Insurance Building.

A. T. Stewart & Co.s, Broadway, from Ninth to Tenth Street.

Trinity Church and Martyrs' Monument.

St. Paul's Chapel—View from Graveyard.

Grace Church, corner of Broadway and Tenth Street.

St. Augustine Chapel, East Houston Street.

St. Patrick's Cathedral, Fifth Avenue

Church, corner of Lexington Avenue and Sixty-third Street

Reformed Dutch Church, Fifth Avenue and Forty-eighth Street.

View of the Bay from the Battery.

Church of the Holy Trinity, Madison Avenue, corner of Forty-second Street.

Synagogue, Lexington Avenue and Fifty-fifth Street.

An Ocean-Steamer outward bound.

Temple Emanuel, corner of Fifth Avenue and Forty-third Street.

St. Bartholomew's, Madison Avenue.

Presbyterian Church, Fifth Avenue and Fifty-fifth Street.

St. Thomas's Church, corner of Fifth Avenue and Fifty-third Street.

East River Bridge, between New York and Brooklyn

Scene on the North River.

St. George's Church, corner of Sixteenth Street and Rutherford Place.

Church of the Transfiguration, Twenty-ninth Street, near Fifth Avenue.

Landing-Steps, west of the Battery.

North River Flotilla

Ferry-Boat at Night.

An Ocean-Steamer in Dock.

North River Oyster-Boats.

The Canal-Boats, East River.

Wharf-Scene.

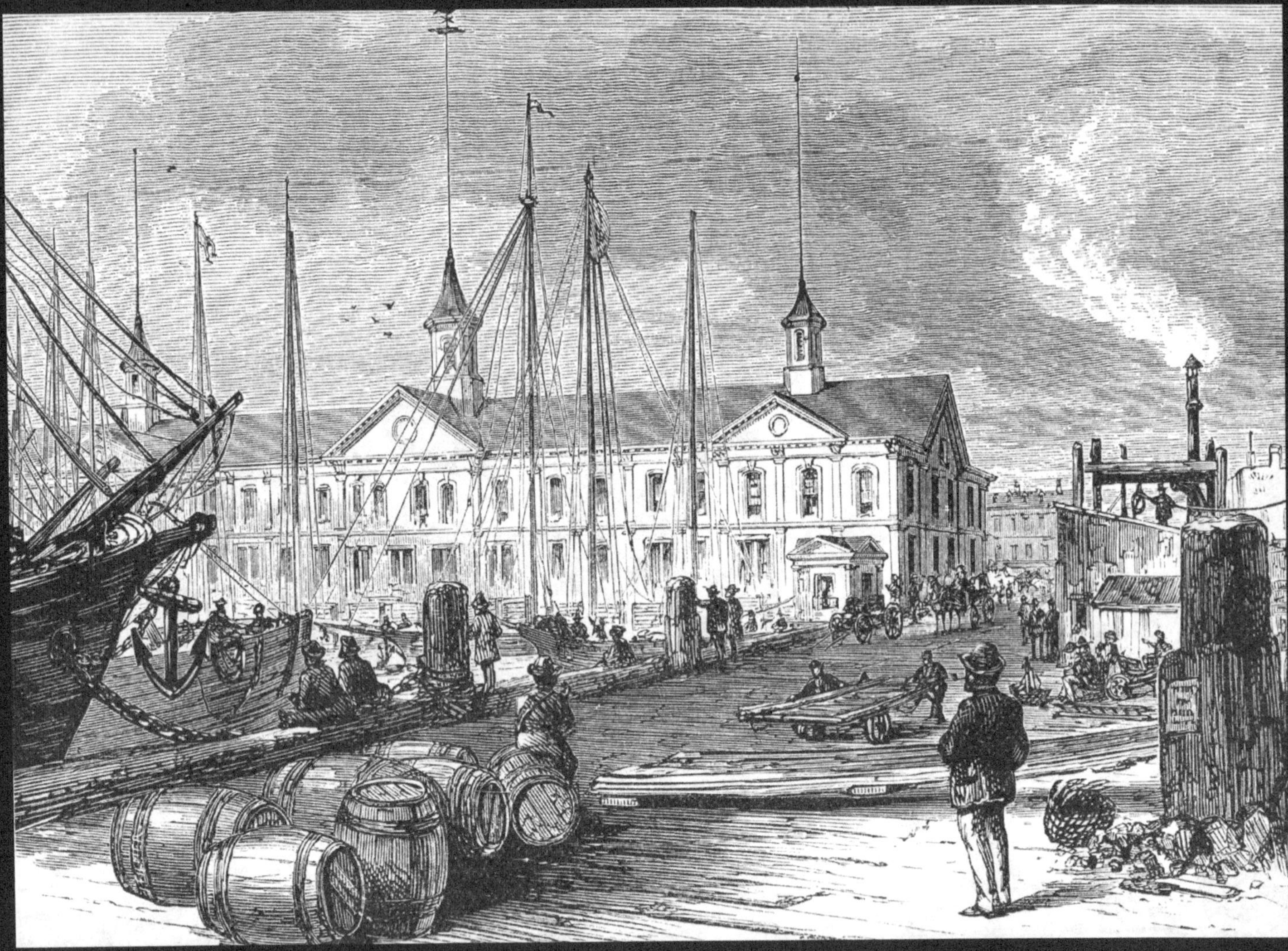

Fish Market, East River.

Fishing-Boats in Dock.

Navy-Yard, Brooklyn.

Dry-Dock.

High Bridge.

Roof and Windows, corner Fifth Avenue and Fifty-seven'h Street.

Façades, Madison Avenue, near Fortieth Street.

Façades, Fifty-seventh Street, between Fifth and Sixth Avenues.

Façades, Fifty-seventh Street, between Fifth and Madison Avenues.

Façade, Columbia College.

Façade, Fifty-seventh Street west of Fifth Avenue.

Porch and Window, Fifty-seventh Street, west of Fifth Avenue.

Porches in Wall Street, below Broad.

Porch of Morse Building, Nassau, corner of Beekman Street.

Porch of Trinity School, Twenty-fifth Street.

Entrance to the Academy of Design.

Porch of Church of Heavenly Rest, Fifth Avenue, near Forty-fifth Street.

Porch of the Dry-Dock Savings-Bank.

Porch in Fifth Avenue.

Porch in East Thirty-sixth Street.

Old-style Doorways.

A Fifth Avenue Porch.

Oriel-Window—Fifth Avenue and Fifty-seventh Street.

Tower—Fifth Avenue and Fifty-seventh Street.

Porch, Thirty-ninth Street, east of Park Avenue.

Mansard-Roof—Fifth Avenue, corner Fifty-sixth Street.

Bay-Window—Fifty-seventh Street, east of Fifth Avenue.

Window—Thirty-fourth Street.

Gable—East Thirty-seventh Street.

Belvedere—Thirty-sixth Street, near Park Avenue.

Tower—Fiftieth Street, near Fifth Avenue.

Tower—Trinity School.

Turret—Fifth Avenue, near Twenty-second Street.

The Obelisk, Central Park.

Harlem River on a Holiday.

Central Park.

Tower—New Court-House, Sixth Avenue.

The Mall, Central Park.

Terrace, Central Park

A. Gibson

Central Park Drives.

Riverside Park.

Jerome Park.

Coney Island as it was.

Scenes at Coney Island.

Scenes at Coney Island.

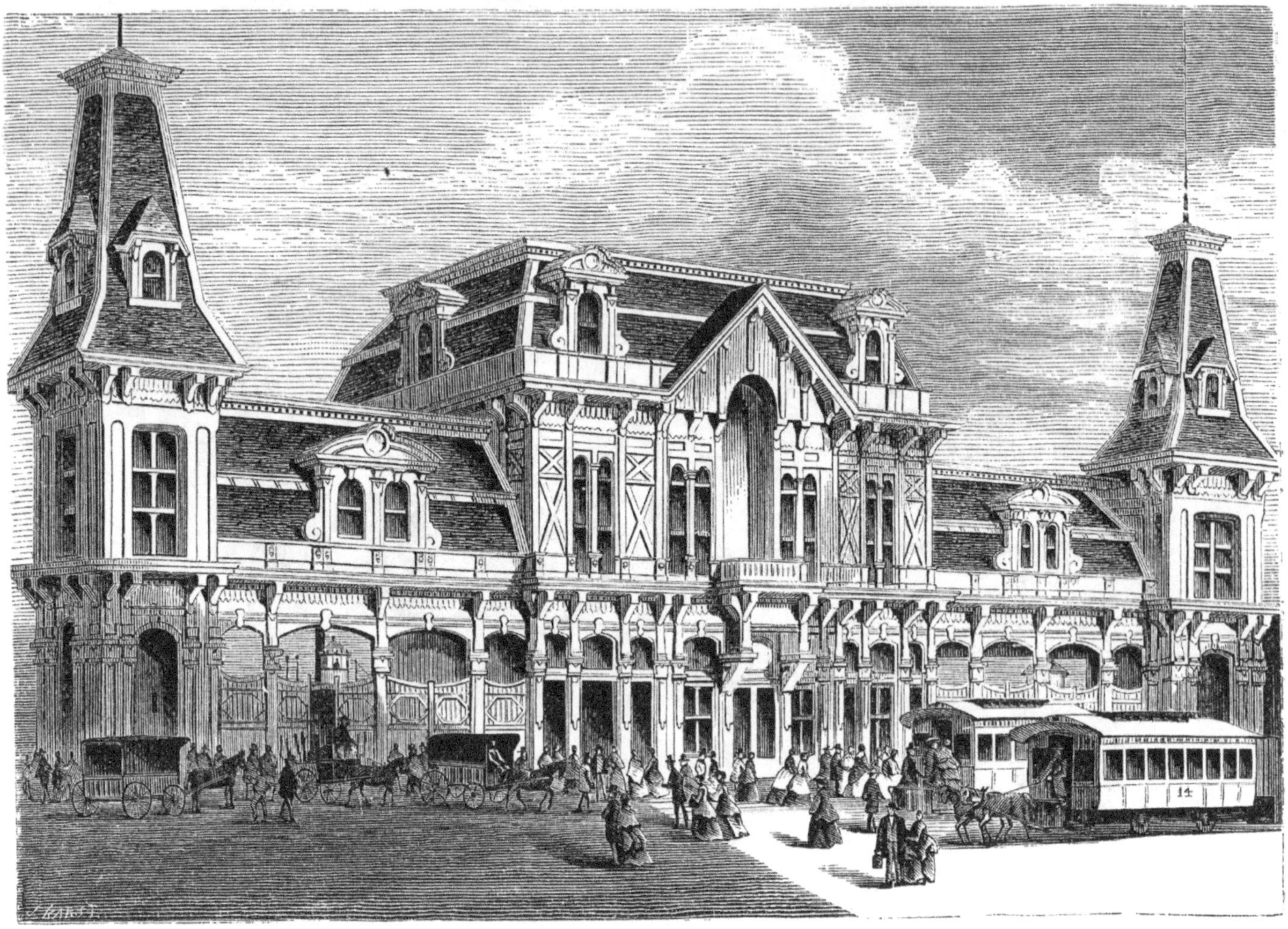

Ferry-House, Brooklyn.

City Hall, with Kings County Court House and Municipal Building in the rear.

Academy of Music and Academy of Design.

Long Island Historical Society Building.

Brooklyn Scenes—Clinton Avenue; Clinton Street; On the Heights.

Prospect Park.

Greenwood Cemetery.

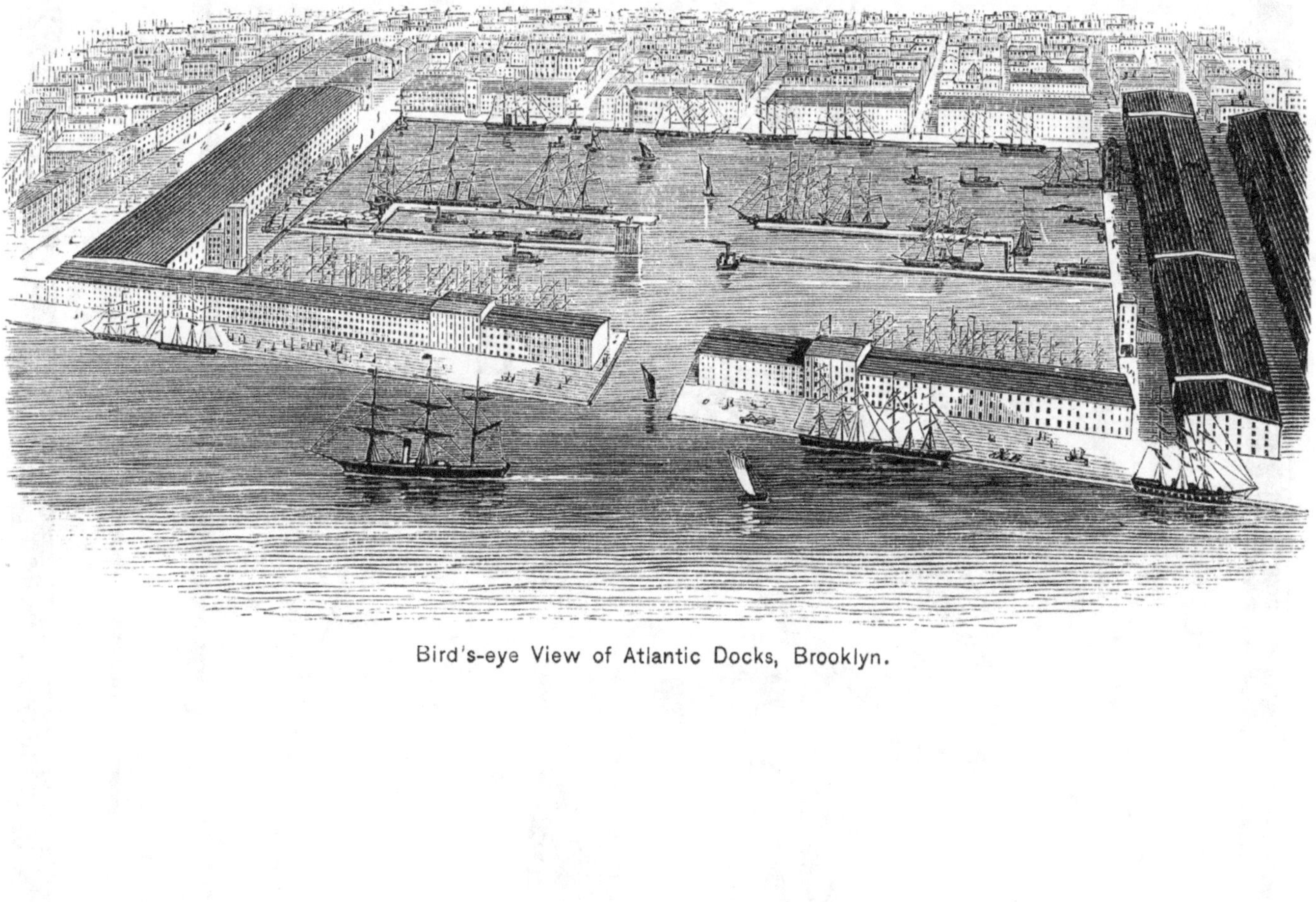

Bird's-eye View of Atlantic Docks, Brooklyn.

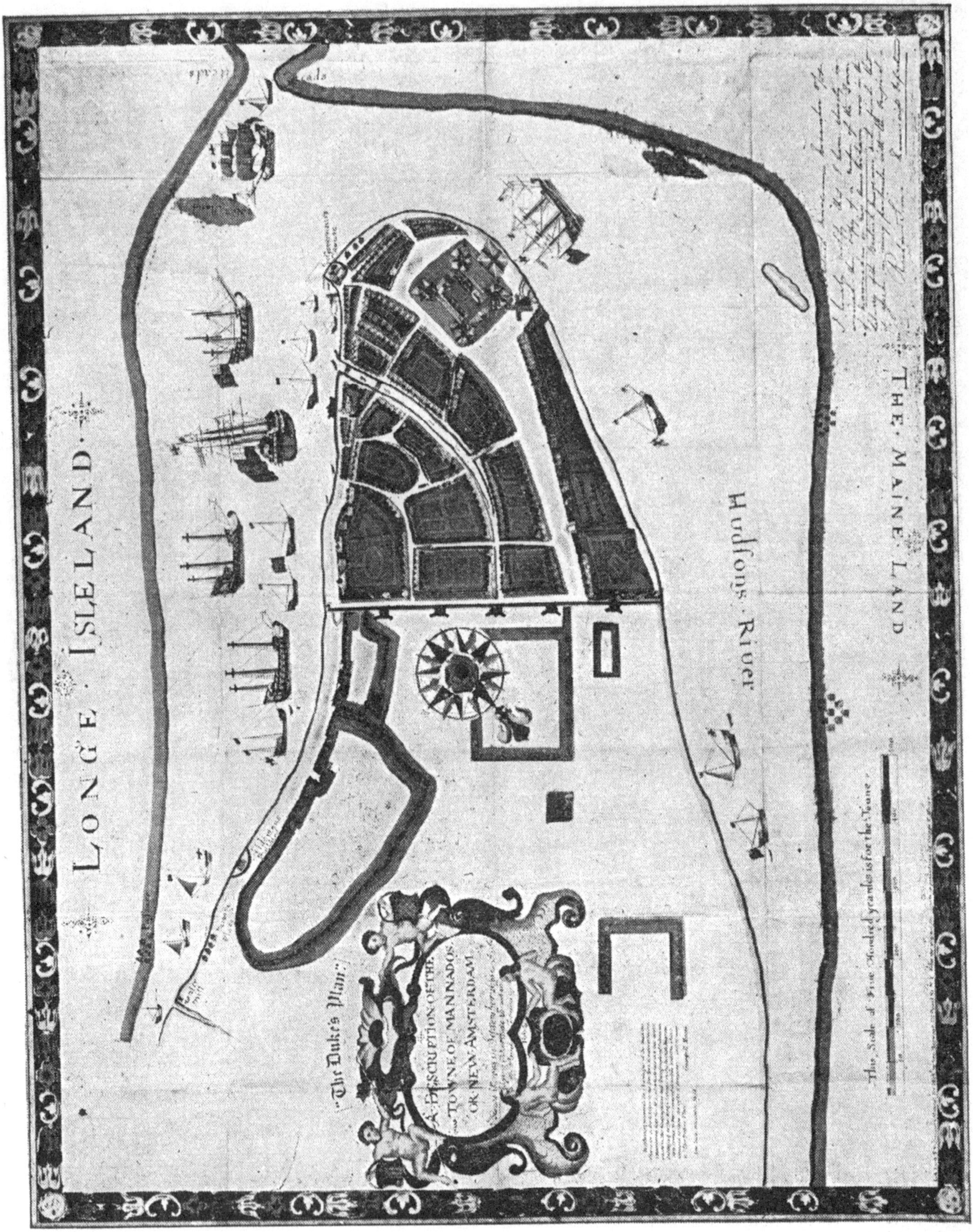

"THE DUKE'S PLAN," MADE FOR JAMES, DUKE OF YORK, ABOUT 1664.

DUTCH COTTAGE AT NEW YORK, 1679.

FACSIMILE of an original Map in the possession of G. H. Smith, Street Commissioner... Pub'd by G. I

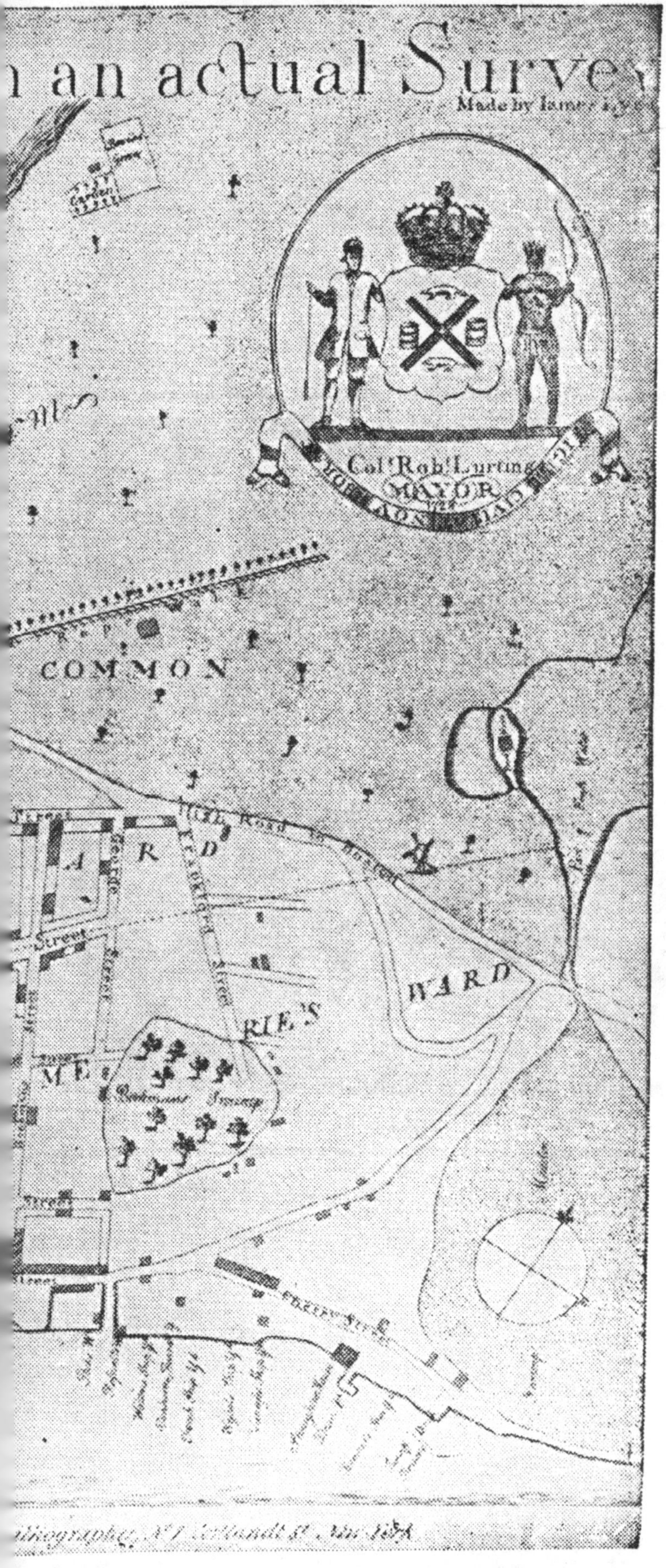

BRADFORD'S MAP OF NEW YORK, 1728.

RHINELANDER'S SUGAR-HOUSE AND RESIDENCE, BETWEEN WILLIAM AND ROSE STREETS.

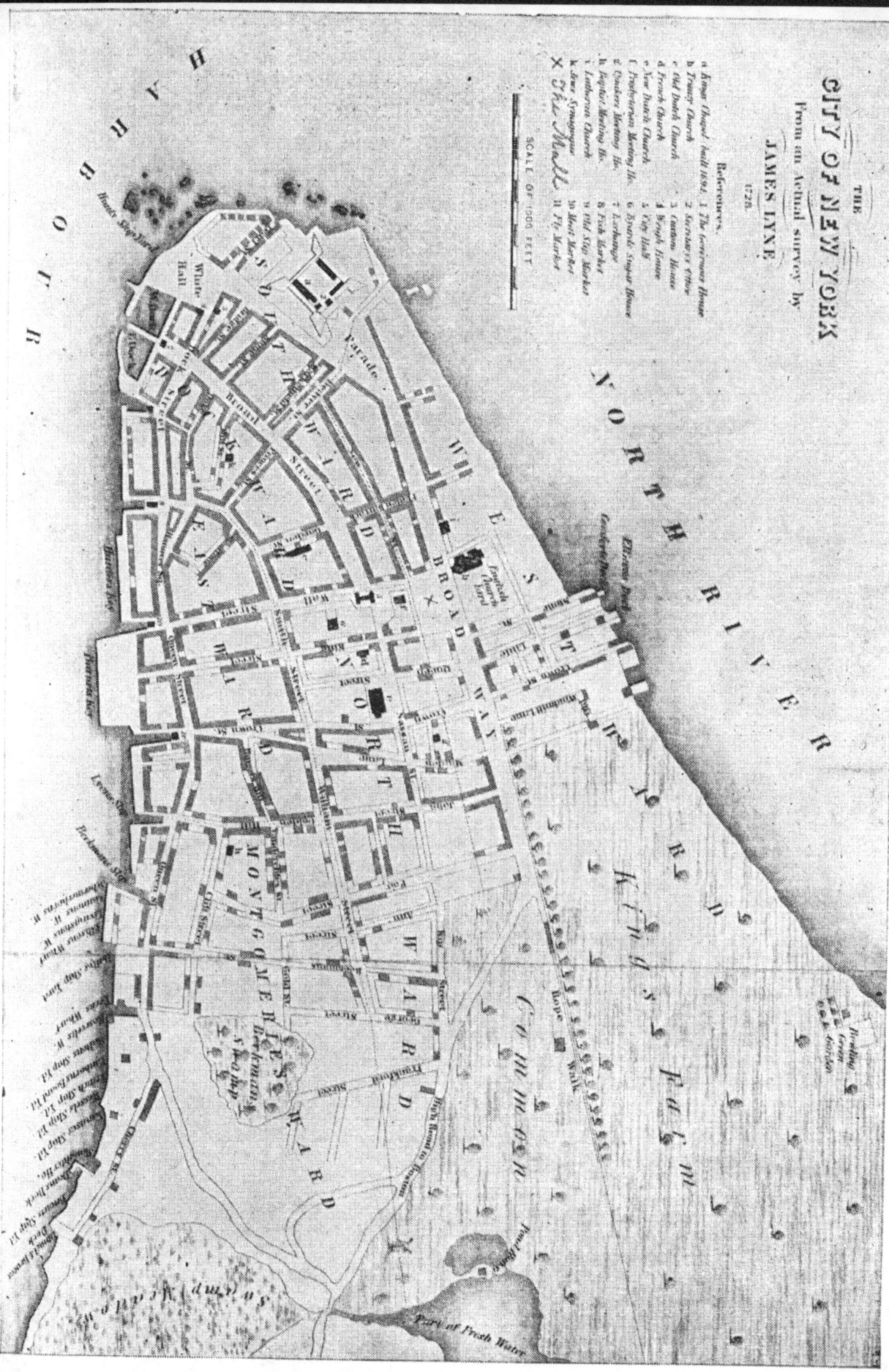

NEW YORK IN 1728, LYNE'S MAP.

THE IRREGULAR PORTION OF THE CITY, AS ORIGINALLY LAID OUT.

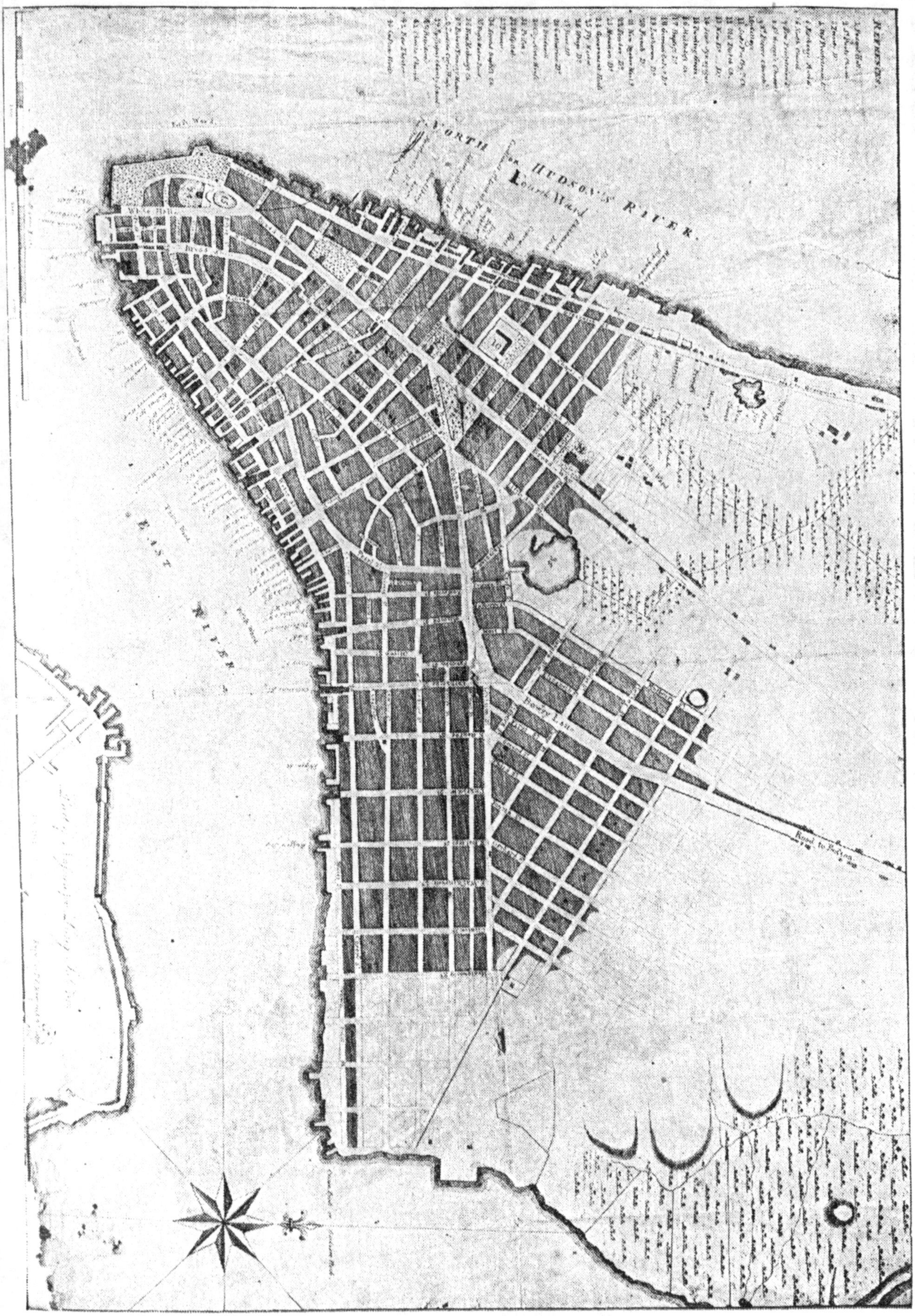

NEW YORK IN 1789. ENGRAVED BY P. R. MAVERICK.

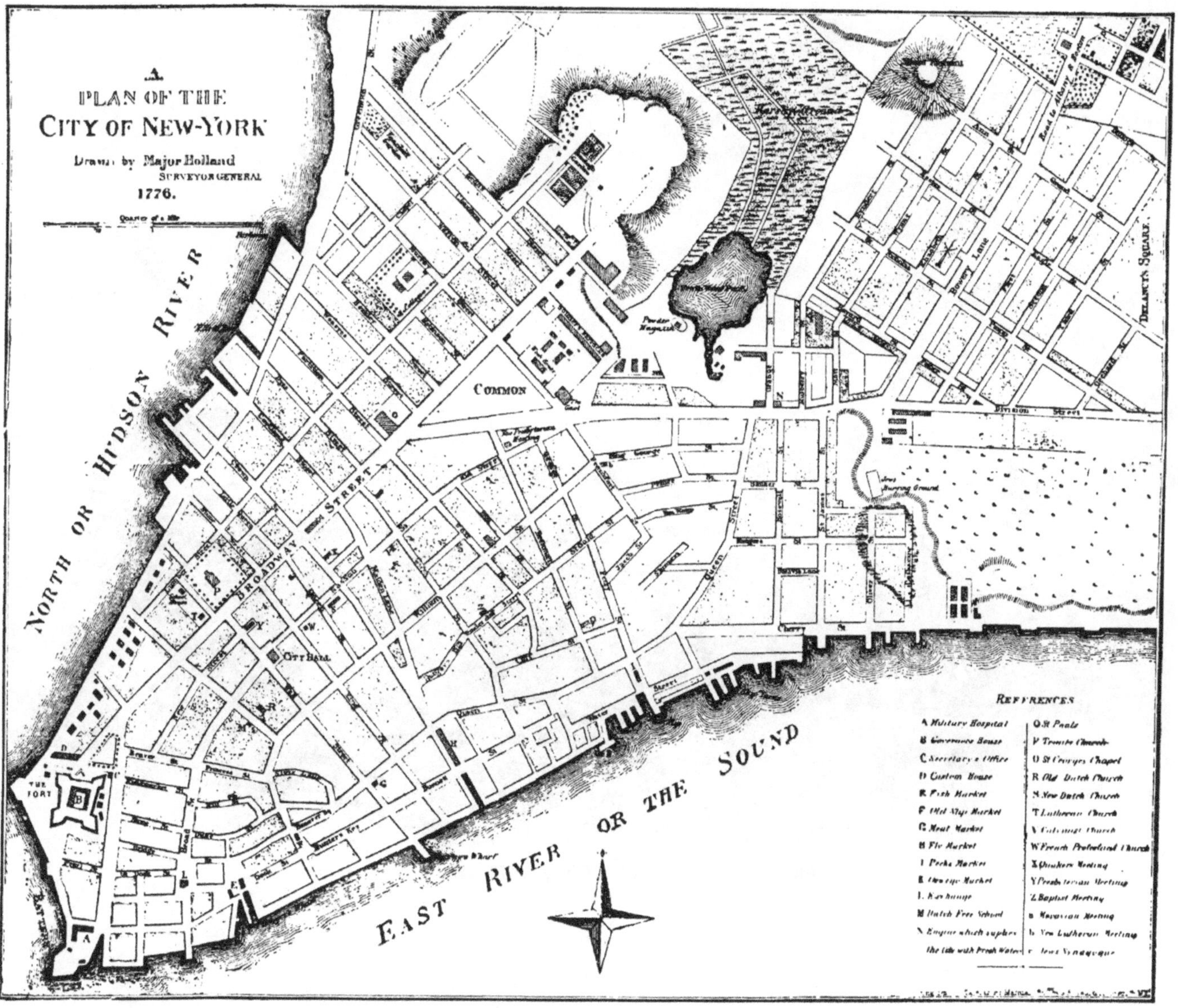

NEW YORK IN 1776. MAJOR HOLLAND'S MAP.

NEW YORK IN 1775. FORT GEORGE, FROM THE HARBOR.

NEW YORK IN 1778. THOMAS KITCHIN, SENIOR'S, MAP. FROM THE LONDON MAGAZINE.

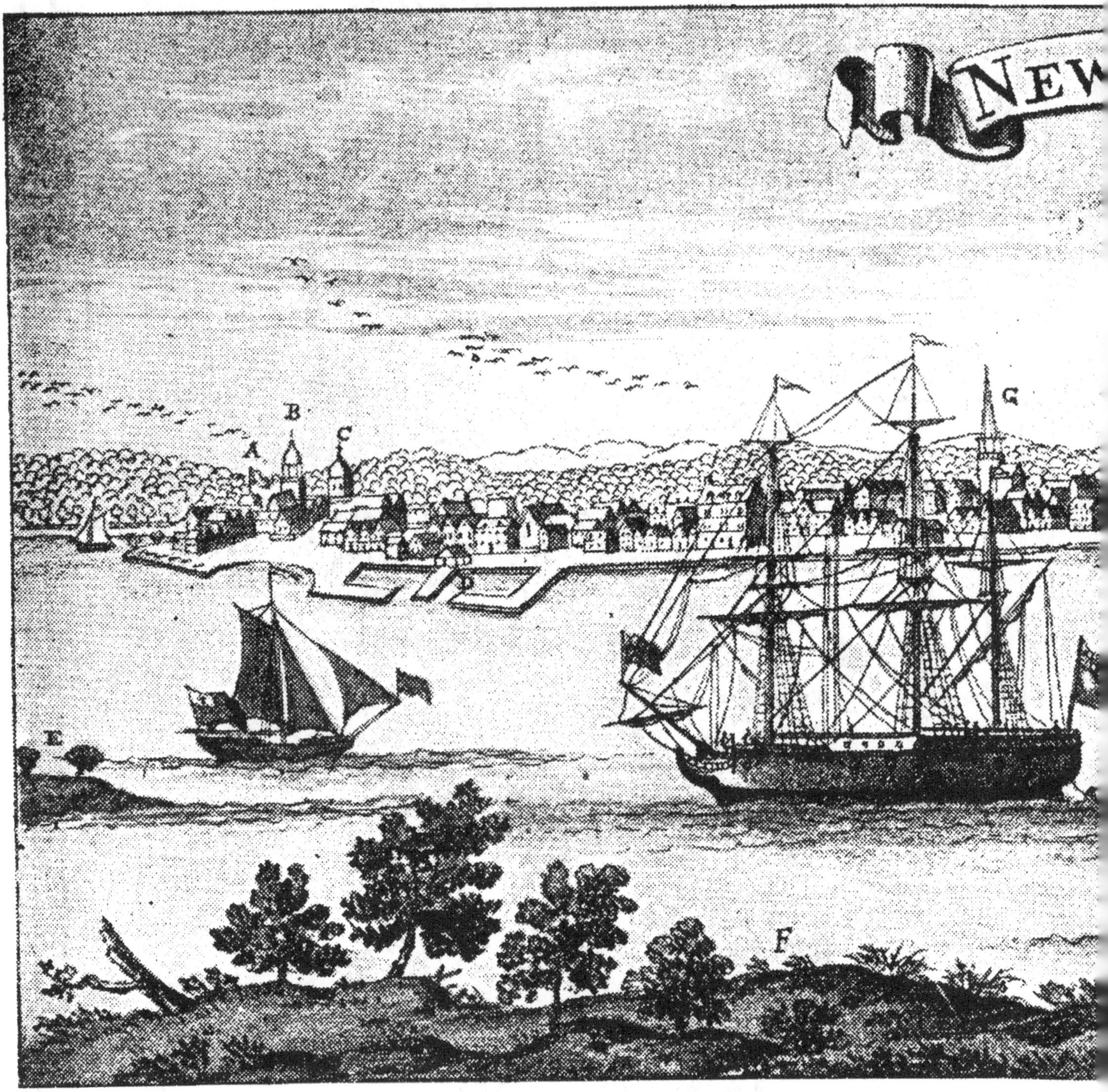

NEW YORK AND EAST RIVER, FROM BROOKLYN HEIGHTS.

ORK
A The Fort
D The Great Dock
F Part of Long Island
G Dutch Church
H English Church
I The City Hall
K The Exchange
L French Church
M Ship Wharfes
I
L
M
N

VIEW OF NEW YORK IN 1746--MIDDLE DUTCH AND FRENCH CHURCHES.

NEW YORK IN 1746--LOWER MARKET AND LANDING.

OLD CITY OR FEDERAL HALL, TRINITY CHURCH AND WALL STREET IN 1789.
ON THE BALCONY OF THIS FEDERAL HALL WASHINGTON WAS MADE PRESIDENT.

JUMEL MANSION, NEAR WASHINGTON HEIGHTS, ONCE WASHINGTON'S HEADQUARTERS.

FRAUNCES' TAVERN, CORNER OF BROAD AND PEARL STREETS

FEDERAL HALL AND PART OF BROAD STREET, 1796.

NEW YORK IN 1805.

BANK OF NEW YORK. MC EVER'S MANSION. CITY BANK.

WALL STREET, BELOW WILLIAM, IN 1800.

THE NEW TRINITY CHURCH AND PART OF WALL STREET.

BROADWAY. ALMS-HOUSE. CITY HALL.

BUILDINGS IN CITY-HALL PARK IN 1809.

RESERVOIR OF MANHATTAN WATER WORKS ON CHAMBERS STREET, IN 1825.

OLD CUSTOM HOUSE AND VICINITY IN 1825.

BROADWAY, FROM BOWLING GREEN, IN 1828.

NORTH BATTERY, AT THE FOOT OF HUBERT STREET.

CITY HALL AND PARK, AND PARK THEATRE.

OLD NEW-YORK POST-OFFICE. SITE OF THE MUTUAL LIFE-INSURANCE BUILDING, ON NASSAU STREET.

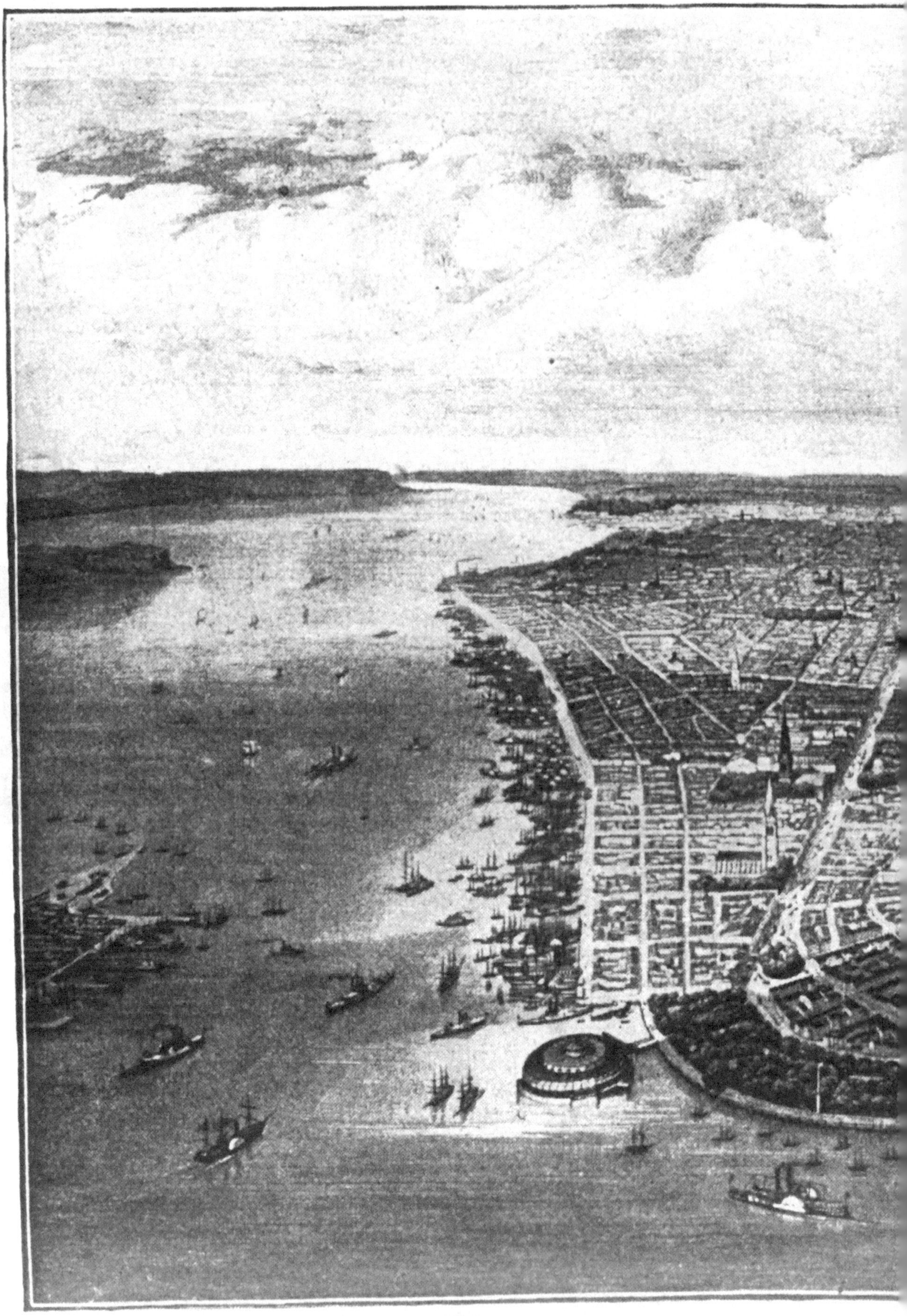

NEW YORK CITY IN 1851.

A REPRODUCTION FROM A LARGE STEEL ENGRAVING.

FIVE POINTS IN 1859, VIEW FROM THE CORNER OF NORTH AND LITTLE WATER STREETS.

VIEW FROM THE SCHOOL-HOUSE IN 42D STREET, BETWEEN SECOND AND THIRD AVENUES, IN 1868.

THE BLIZZARD OF MARCH 11TH, 12TH, AND 13TH, 1888.
PHOTOGRAPHS TAKEN JUST AFTER THE STORM, BY LANGILL.

WASHINGTON CENTENNIAL EXERCISES IN 1889, AT THE UNITED-STATES SUB-TREASURY.

PHOTOGRAPHED BY JOHNSTON, WHILE THE REV. DR. R. S. STORRS WAS OFFERING PRAYER.

THE LOEW BRIDGE, BROADWAY AND FULTON STREET.

PRODUCE EXCHANGE TOWER. "TRIBUNE." "TIMES."

NEW-YORK CITY.

LOOKING SOUTHWEST FROM THE "WORLD" DOME.

"TIMES." ST. PAUL'S. POST OFFICE. CITY-HALL PARK.

NEW-YORK CITY.

LOOKING WEST FROM THE "WORLD" DOME.

MURRAY STREET. CITY HALL. WARREN STREET.

NEW-YORK CITY.

LOOKING WEST-NORTHWEST FROM THE "WORLD" DOME.

MURRAY STREET. CITY HALL. WARREN STREET.

NEW-YORK CITY.

LOOKING WEST-NORTHWEST FROM THE "WORLD" DOME.

CITY-HALL PARK. COUNTY COURT-HOUSE. COURT OF GENERAL SESSIONS.

NEW-YORK CITY.

LOOKING NORTH FROM THE "WORLD" DOME.

COURT OF GENERAL SESSIONS. POLICE COURT. CENTRE STREET. "STAATS ZEITUNG."

NEW-YORK CITY.

LOOKING NORTHEAST FROM THE "WORLD" DOME.

"STAATS ZEITUNG."　　CITY-HALL BRANCH ELEVATED RAILROAD.　　WILLIAM STREET.

NEW-YORK CITY.

LOOKING EAST-NORTHEAST FROM THE "WORLD" DOME.

NEWSBOY'S LODGING-HOUSE.

APPROACH TO BROOKLYN BRIDGE.

NEW-YORK CITY.

LOOKING EAST-SOUTHEAST FROM THE "WORLD" DOME.

SHOT TOWER. SPRUCE AND WILLIAM STREETS.

NEW-YORK CITY.

LOOKING SOUTH FROM THE "WORLD" DOME.

NEW-YORK CITY.

LOOKING SOUTH-SOUTHWEST FROM THE "WORLD" DOME.

NEW-YORK HARBOR, FROM EAST-RIVER BRIDGE, IN 1893.

UNITED-STATES BARGE OFFICE, BATTERY PLACE.

BAY AND HARBOR FROM BEDLOE'S ISLAND, ABOUT 1840.

HELL GATE, FROM GREAT BARN ISLAND, ABOUT 1825.

AMERICAN LINE, NEW PIERS 14 AND 15, NORTH RIVER.

PECK SLIP, EAST RIVER.

ELLIS-ISLAND IMMIGRANT STATION, IN NEW-YORK HARBOR.

THE LANDING-PLACE FOR IMMIGRANTS.

SOUTH STREET AND HARBOR, AND JEANNETTEE PARK.

NEW-YORK CENTRAL & HUDSON-RIVER RAILROAD COMPANY'S ELEVATOR.

HOBOKEN FERRY PIER, NORTH RIVER, FOOT OF CHRISTOPHER STREET.

NORTH GERMAN LLOYD STEAMSHIP COMPANY.
PIERS AT HOBOKEN. OFFICES AT 2 BOWLING GREEN, NEW YORK

NORTH GERMAN LLOYD STEAMSHIP COMPANY.
PIERS AT HOBOKEN. OFFICES AT 2 BOWLING GREEN, NEW YORK

HAMBURG-AMERICAN PACKET COMPANY.

PIERS AT HOBOKEN. OFFICES AT 37 BROADWAY, NEW YORK.

RED STAR LINE STEAMSHIP "FRIESLAND." OFFICES, 6 BOWLING GREEN.

RED STAR LINE STEAMSHIP "WESTERNLAND," OFFICES, 6 BOWLING GREEN.

NETHERLANDS-AMERICAN LINE STEAMSHIP "SPAARNDAM," OFFICE 39 BROADWAY, PIER IN HOBOKEN.

CLYDE'S STEAMSHIP PIER, AT FOOT OF ROOSEVELT STREET, NEW YORK.

OCEAN STEAMSHIP CO. OF SAVANNAH (SAVANNAH LINE), PIERS 34 AND 35, NORTH RIVER, FOOT OF SPRING AND CANAL STREETS.

MALLORY S. S. LINES. NEW-YORK & TEXAS S. S. CO., PIERS 20 AND 21 EAST RIVER.

FORT WADSWORTH, THE SCHOOL SHIP AND WAR-VESSELS.

VIEWS TAKEN IN NORTH RIVER AND NEW-YORK HARBOR. PHOTOS BY JOHNSTON.

ATLAS MAIL LINE TO THE WEST INDIES, PIER 55, NORTH RIVER.

HUDSON RIVER STEAMER "ALBANY."

HUDSON-RIVER DAY LINE STEAMERS, "NEW YORK" AND "ALBANY," DESBROSSES-STREET PIER, N. R.

CENTRAL PARK. THE NEW NETHERLAND. THE SAVOY. THE PLAZA. THE DALHOUSIE.

58TH STREET, LOOKING EAST FROM SIXTH AVENUE.

RAMSDELL LINE TO NEWBURGH: HOMER RAMSDELL TRANSPORTATION CO., FOOT OF FRANKLIN ST., NORTH RIVER.

FULTON FERRY, FOOT OF FULTON STREET, EAST RIVER.

NEW-YORK CENTRAL & HUDSON-RIVER RAILROAD TRACKS ABOVE 98TH STREET.

EAST RIVER --- THE BROOKLYN BRIDGE --- SOUTH STREET.

JEANETTE PARK, COENTIES SLIP, EAST RIVER, LOOKING TOWARD BROOKLYN, SHOWING THE CANAL-BOAT FLEET.

BIRD'S-EYE VIEW FROM WASHINGTON BUILDING, LOOKING SOUTHWEST.

BIRD'S-EYE VIEW FROM WASHINGTON BUILDING LOOKING SOUTHEAST.

GRAND CENTRAL RAILROAD STATION,
42D STREET AND VANDERBILT AVENUE.

"EMPIRE-STATE EXPRESS," NEW-YORK CENTRAL & HUDSON-RIVER RAILROAD.
FASTEST LONG-DISTANCE TRAIN IN THE WORLD. PHOTO. BY A. P. YATES, OF SYRACUSE, N. Y.

MOTT-HAVEN STATION, 138TH STREET, NEW-YORK CENTRAL & HUDSON-RIVER RAILROAD.

MORRISANIA STATION, NEW-YORK CENTRAL & HUDSON-RIVER RAILROAD.

SWITCH TOWER CONTROLLING ALL TRAINS ENTERING THE GRAND CENTRAL DEPOT.

PENNSYLVANIA RAILROAD. JERSEY-CITY STATION.

PENNSYLVANIA RAILROAD: FREIGHT DEPOT, WEST STREET.

MOTT-HAVEN CANAL.

SOUTHERN PACIFIC COMPANY -- "MORGAN LINE," -- PIER 25, NORTH RIVER.

PENNSYLVANIA RAILROAD DEPOT, JERSEY CITY, INTERIOR OF TRAIN-HOUSE.

READING RAILROAD SYSTEM -- LEHIGH VALLEY DIVISION. DEPOT IN JERSEY CITY.

WEST STREET, FOOT OF LIBERTY STREET.

TRAIN-HOUSE OF THE GRAND CENTRAL STATION, ON 42D STREET.

CENTRAL BUILDING: CENTRAL RAILROAD OF NEW JERSEY, LIBERTY AND WEST STREETS, NEW YORK.

DELAWARE, LACKAWANNA & WESTERN RAILROAD: DEPOT IN HOBOKEN.

ELEVATED RAILROAD NEAR COENTIES SLIP, EAST RIVER.

DELAWARE, LACKAWANNA & WESTERN RAILROAD COMPANY.
GENERAL OFFICES: EXCHANGE PLACE AND WILLIAM STREET.

ELEVATED RAILROAD, AT COENTIES SLIP. PRODUCE EXCHANGE TOWER.

CONEY ISLAND, NEW YORK'S HOLIDAY RESORT.

DESBROSSES-STREET FERRY AND PASSENGER-STATION, WEST STREET, NORTH RIVER.

A NORTH-RIVER FERRY BOAT.

DELAWARE & HUDSON CANAL COMPANY.
COMPANY'S BUILDING, CALLED "THE COAL AND IRON EXCHANGE," CORTLANDT AND CHURCH STREETS.

SOUTH-FERRY STATION--ELEVATED RAILROAD.

ELEVATED RAILROAD AT 110TH STREET AND NINTH AVENUE.

FIFTH-AVENUE STAGE AT THE CATHEDRAL.

CABLE-CARS ON THE EAST-RIVER BRIDGE, NEW-YORK END.

BATTERY PLACE--WASHINGTON BUILDING. PRODUCE EXCHANGE.

PASSENGER ELEVATOR AND STATION, ELEVATED RAILROAD,
EIGHTH AVENUE AND 116TH STREET.

WHITEHALL STREET, LOOKING TOWARDS BROADWAY.   ARMY BUILDING.

PRODUCE EXCHANGE. STEAMSHIP ROW, BOWLING GREEN. STATE STREET

LOWER BROADWAY, LOOKING NORTH, FROM MORRIS STREET TO TRINITY CHURCH.

BROADWAY AND FIFTH AVENUE, SOUTH FROM MADISON SQUARE.

BROADWAY AND SIXTH AVENUE, NORTH FROM 34TH STREET.

FOURTEENTH STREET, BETWEEN FIFTH AND SIXTH AVENUES.

BROADWAY, FROM PARK PLACE TO CHAMBERS STREET.

OPPOSITE CITY-HALL PARK.

MRS. WILLIAM H. VANDERBILT. WILLIAM D. SLOANE. MRS. ELLIOTT F. SHEPARD. WILLIAM K. VANDERBILT. ST. THOMAS CHURCH. DR. HALL'S CHURCH.

FIFTH AVENUE, LOOKING NORTH FROM 51st STREET.

SHOWING THE VANDERBILT RESIDENCES, AND ST. THOMAS EPISCOPAL AND THE FIFTH-AVENUE PRESBYTERIAN CHURCHES.

THE CHARLES L. TIFFANY RESIDENCE.

MADISON AVENUE, NORTHWEST CORNER OF SEVENTY-SECOND STREET.

NEWSPAPER ROW. ST. PAUL'S CHURCH. POST OFFICE.

PARK ROW, LOOKING SOUTH FROM MAIL STREET.

UNION SQUARE. WASHINGTON MONUMENT.

FOURTH AVENUE, LOOKING NORTH FROM UNION SQUARE.

ST. BARTHOLOMEW'S CHURCH. MANHATTAN ATHLETIC CLUB. HOLY TRINITY CHURCH.

MADISON AVENUE, LOOKING NORTH FROM 42D STREET.

PRESBYTERIAN HOSPITAL. CHARLES F. CLARK. JOHN KING.

MADISON AVENUE, EAST SIDE, BETWEEN 69TH AND 70TH STREETS.

HARLEM VIEW, LOOKING EAST FROM 137TH STREET.

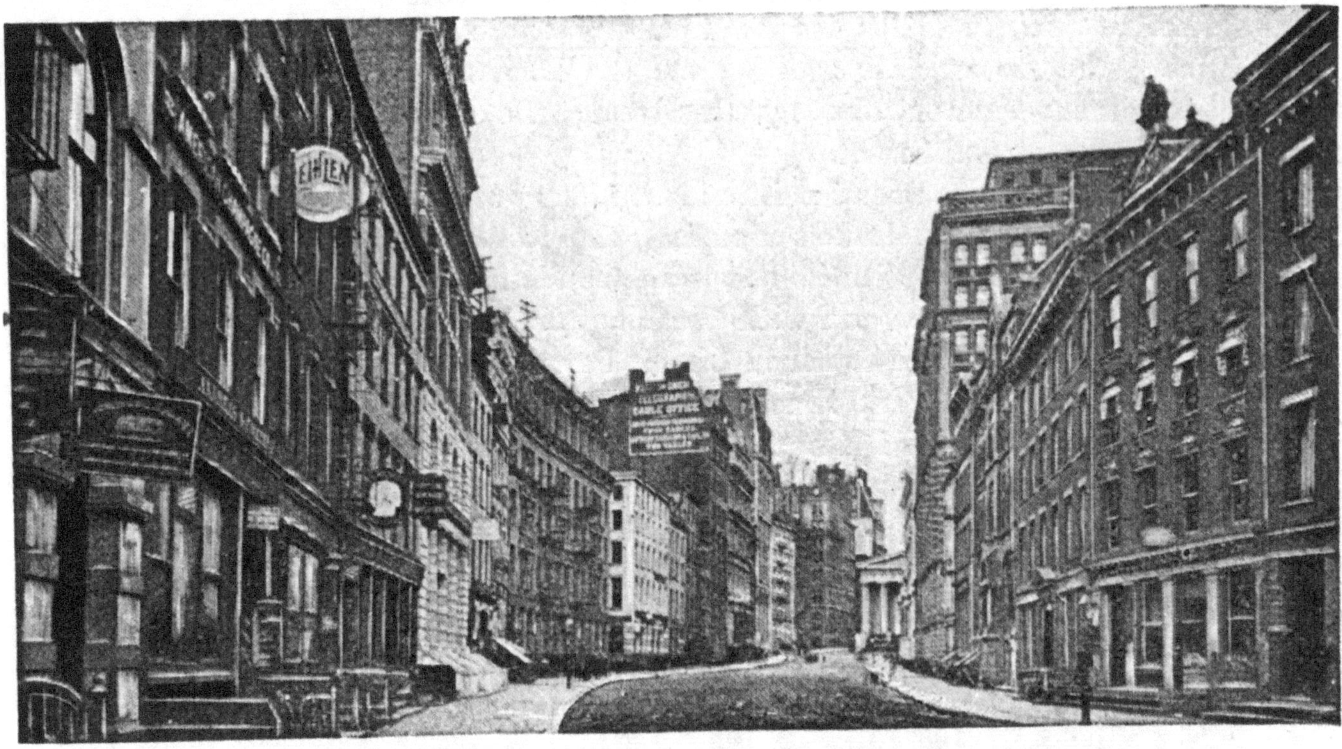

EDISON BUILDING. STOCK EXCHANGE. MILLS BUILDING.

BROAD STREET, NORTH TO WALL STREET.

JEANNETTE PARK, COENTIES SLIP.

SOUTH STREET, NORTH FROM THE BATTERY.

BROAD STREET, SOUTH FROM WALL STREET.

WALKER STREET.--HARRY HOWARD SQUARE.--CANAL STREET.

"CHINATOWN"--MOTT STREET, WEST OF PARK ROW.

JOHN DWIGHT & CO.

FACTORIES: FIRST AVENUE AND EAST 112TH STREET. OFFICES: 11 OLD SLIP.

BROADWAY, FROM THE BROADWAY CENTRAL HOTEL TO GRACE CHURCH.
BOND STREET TO TENTH STREET.

MULBERRY BEND, THE ITALIAN QUARTER.

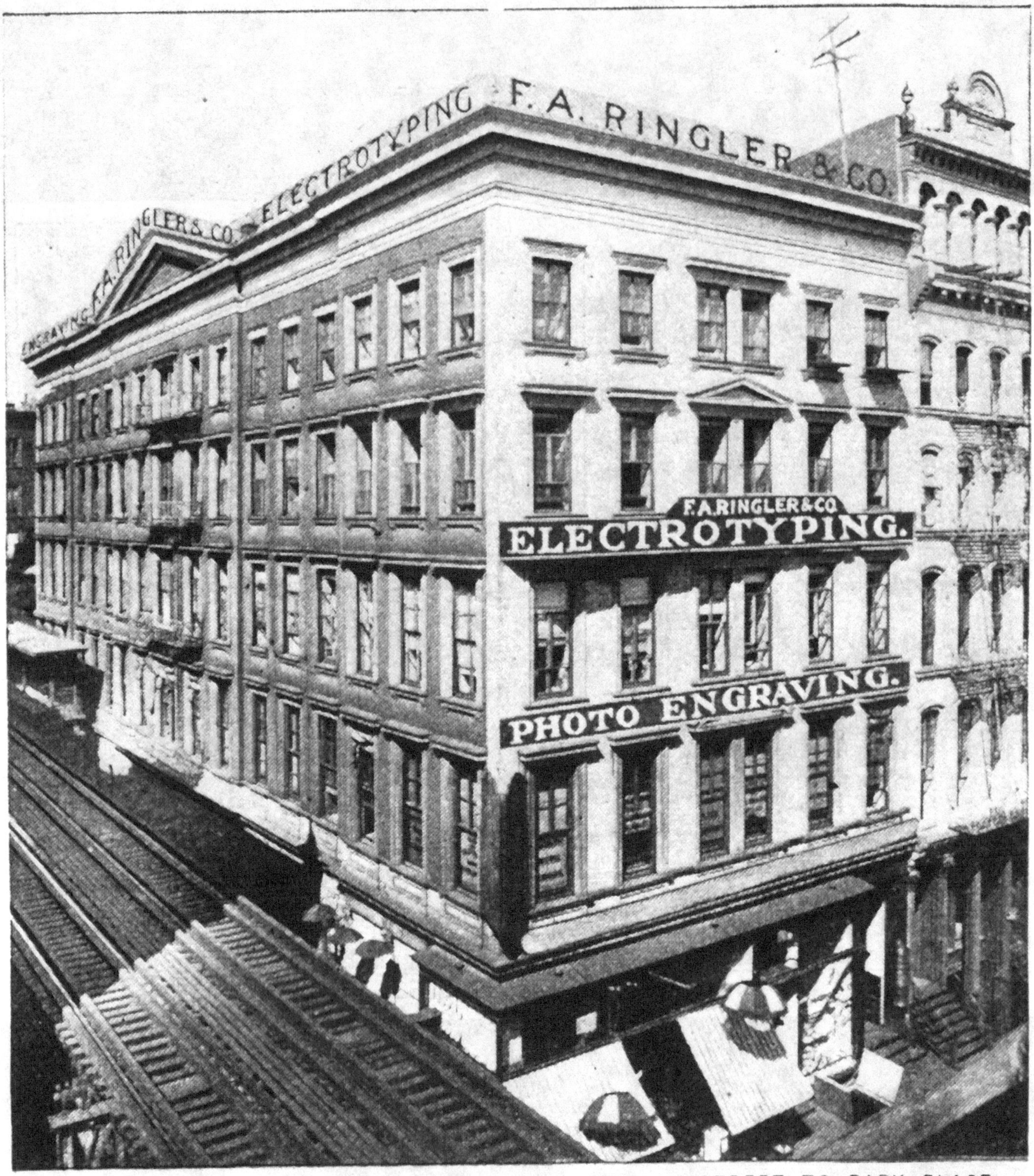

F. A. RINGLER CO., CHURCH STREET, FROM BARCLAY STREET TO PARK PLACE.

TERRACE, FOUNTAIN AND LAKE, IN CENTRAL PARK.

BOAT-HOUSE AND LAKE IN CENTRAL PARK.

SCENES AND ORNAMENTAL STRUCTURES.
IN CENTRAL PARK.

STATUES, BUSTS AND ORNAMENTS.

IN CENTRAL PARK.

STATUES AND ORNAMENTAL WORK.

IN CENTRAL PARK.

MENAGERIE IN CENTRAL PARK.

BOW BRIDGE, IN CENTRAL PARK.

STATUES AND BUSTS.
IN CENTRAL PARK.

THE CAVE, LAKE, OLD FORT, AND ORNAMENTAL STRUCTURES.
IN CENTRAL PARK.

WASHINGTON MEMORIAL ARCH.

WASHINGTON SQUARE, BEGINNING OF FIFTH AVENUE. JUDSON MEMORIAL CHURCH SHOWS THROUGH THE ARCH.

WASHINGTON SQUARE AND WASHINGTON ARCH.

MOUNT MORRIS PARK, FIFTH AVENUE, 120TH TO 124TH STREETS.

LIBERTY ENLIGHTENING THE WORLD.

STATUE, BY BARTHOLDI, ON BEDLOE'S ISLAND, NEW-YORK HARBOR.

F. A. FERRIS & COMPANY PACKING ESTABLISHMENT.

MOTT STREET, EAST SIDE, BETWEEN HOUSTON AND PRINCE STREETS.

DODGE STATUE, AT BROADWAY AND SIXTH AVENUE.

R. HOE & CO. PRINTING-PRESS AND SAW WORKS.
GRAND, BROOME, COLUMBIA AND SHERIFF STREETS, NEAR EAST RIVER.

COLUMBUS STATUE, 59TH STREET, BROADWAY AND EIGHTH AVENUE.

NEW-YORK BISCUIT COMPANY.

TENTH AVENUE, FROM 15TH STREET TO 16TH STREET.

EAST RIVER, OR NEW-YORK AND BROOKLYN, BRIDGE.

ACROSS THE EAST RIVER FROM NEW YORK TO BROOKLYN.

BROOKLYN BRIDGE PROMENADE -- LOOKING TOWARD NEW-YORK.

THE MECHANICAL RUBBER COMPANY, 13 AND 15 PARK ROW.

THE WASHINGTON BRIDGE, ACROSS THE HARLEM RIVER.
FROM 181ST STREET AND TENTH AVENUE TO AQUEDUCT AVENUE.

HIGH BRIDGE (OR "CROTON AQUEDUCT BRIDGE"), ACROSS THE HARLEM RIVER.
AT 175TH STREET AND TENTH AVENUE.

APPROACH TO THE WASHINGTON BRIDGE.

THIRD-AVENUE, OR HARLEM, BRIDGE.

SUBURBAN ELEVATED RAILWAY BRIDGE, AT SECOND AVENUE AND 129TH STREET.

HARLEM RIVER AND HARLEM BRIDGE, AT 130TH STREET AND THIRD AVENUE.

PARK AVENUE, NORTH FROM 98TH STREET. N. Y. C. & H. R. R. R. TRACKS.

HARLEM RIVER AND SECOND AVENUE BRIDGE, AT 129TH STREET.

HIGH SERVICE STATION, 98TH STREET, NEAR COLUMBUS AVENUE.

EDISON ELECTRIC ILLUMINATING CO., 26TH STREET, BETWEEN BROADWAY AND SIXTH AVENUE.

GATE HOUSE, CROTON AQUEDUCT.
MANHATTAN AVENUE AND 135TH STREET.

RESERVOIR, FIFTH AVENUE, 40TH AND 42D STREETS.

EDISON ELECTRIC ILLUMINATING CO., PEARL AND ELM STREETS.

GENERAL ELECTRIC COMPANY.

EDISON BUILDING, 42 AND 44 BROAD STREET, BETWEEN EXCHANGE PLACE AND BEAVER STREET.

BAXTER STREET.
ONE PHASE OF LIFE IN THE METROPOLIS.

BROADWAY AND DEY STREET.

SHOWING MERCANTILE NATIONAL BANK, WESTERN UNION TELEGRAPH BUILDING, AND "THE MAIL AND EXPRESS."

THE STANDARD OIL COMPANY.
STANDARD OIL CO.'S BUILDING, 26 BROADWAY, OPPOSITE BOWLING GREEN.

METROPOLITAN TELEPHONE AND TELEGRAPH COMPANY.
TELEPHONE BUILDING, CORTLANDT STREET, BETWEEN BROADWAY AND CHURCH STREET.

TELEPHONE OPERATING OR SWITCH-ROOM, ON CORTLANDT ST., METROPOLITAN TELEPHONE AND TELEGRAPH CO.

METROPOLITAN TELEPHONE AND TELEGRAPH CO., BROAD AND PEARL STREETS.

HOTEL WALDORF.

FIFTH AVENUE, NORTHWEST CORNER OF 33D STREET.

HOTEL NEW NETHERLAND.

FIFTH AVENUE, NORTHEAST CORNER OF 59TH STREET, AT MAIN ENTRANCE TO CENTRAL PARK.

HOTEL SAVOY.

FIFTH AVENUE, SOUTHEAST CORNER 59TH STREET, OPPOSITE MAIN ENTRANCE TO CENTRAL PARK.

THE PLAZA HOTEL.

AT FIFTH-AVENUE ENTRANCE TO CENTRAL PARK.

HOLLAND HOUSE.

FIFTH AVENUE, SOUTHWEST CORNER OF THIRTIETH STREET.

HOTEL GRENOBLE, SEVENTH AVENUE, FROM 56TH STREET TO 57TH STREET.

PARK-AVENUE HOTEL, PARK AVENUE, FROM 32D STREET TO 33D STREET.

HOTEL CAMBRIDGE, FIFTH AVENUE AND 33D STREET.

GRAND UNION HOTEL, FOURTH AVENUE, FROM 41st STREET TO 42d STREET, OPPOSITE GRAND CENTRAL DEPOT.

HARLEM RIVER, LOOKING EAST FROM WASHINGTON BRIDGE.

EAST RIVER BRIDGE, FROM NEAR THE BROOKLYN LANDING.

WESTMINSTER HOTEL, IRVING PLACE AND 16TH STREET, NEAR UNION SQUARE.

BROADWAY CENTRAL HOTEL, BROADWAY, OPPOSITE BOND STREET.

DELMONICO'S : FIFTH AVENUE, BROADWAY AND 26TH STREET.

DELMONICO'S.

BEAVER AND WILLIAM STREETS, OPPOSITE THE COTTON EXCHANGE.

BROADWAY, LOOKING NORTH FROM BARCLAY STREET. THE POST OFFICE.

PARK PLACE, FROM BROADWAY TO CHURCH STREET.

OTIS BROTHERS & CO.'S ELEVATOR WORKS.

MANUFACTORY AT YONKERS. NEW-YORK OFFICES AT 38 PARK ROW.

ELEVATOR WORKS

POST OFFICE. WORLD, TIMES AND POTTER BUILDINGS. PARK ROW. ANN STREET.

JEFFERSON-MARKET POLICE-COURT, SIXTH AND GREENWICH AVENUES.

NINETEENTH-WARD POLICE-COURT, 191 EAST 57TH STREET.

LUDLOW-STREET JAIL. ESSEX-MARKET COURT.

ESSEX-MARKET POLICE-COURT, ESSEX ST. AND ESSEX-MARKET PLACE.

THE CRIMINAL LAW COURTS (UNFINISHED) AND THE TOMBS.

CENTRE STREET, WEST SIDE, FROM FRANKLIN TO LEONARD STREETS.

THE CITY HALL.

IN CITY-HALL PARK, OPPOSITE MURRAY STREET, BETWEEN BROADWAY AND PARK ROW.

THE COUNTY COURT-HOUSE.

BROADWAY AND CHAMBERS STREET, IN CITY-HALL PARK.

THE UNITED-STATES POST OFFICE, BROADWAY, PARK ROW AND MAIL STREET.

SIEGEL BROTHERS, 65 AND 67 WOOSTER STREET.

NORMAL COLLEGE.

PARK AND LEXINGTON AVENUES, EAST 68TH AND EAST 69TH STREETS.

TEFFT, WELLER & COMPANY.

320, 322, 824, 326, 328 AND 330 BROADWAY, EAST SIDE, BETWEEN PEARL AND WORTH STREETS.

14TH STREET, FROM UNIVERSITY PLACE TO FIFTH AVENUE.

14TH STREET AND BROADWAY, LOOKING TOWARDS GRACE CHURCH.

UNIVERSITY OF THE CITY OF NEW YORK, WASHINGTON SQUARE, EAST, AND WAVERLY PLACE.

BROADWAY AND 29TH STREET, SHOWING IMPERIAL MUSIC HALL AND DALY'S THEATRE.

LEXINGTON AVENUE AND 63D STREET, SHOWING RODOPH SHOLOM SYNAGOGUE.

METROPOLITAN POLICE ANNUAL PARADE REVIEWED BY INFANTA EULALIA IN MADISON SQUARE.

FOOT OF WHITEHALL STREET AND GOVERNOR'S ISLAND, FROM ARMY BUILDING.

STUYVESANT PLACE, 8TH STREET AND ST. MARK'S PLACE, EAST FROM THIRD AVENUE.

UNION SQUARE, LOOKING TOWARDS THE NORTHWEST.

BROADWAY, SIXTH AVENUE AND 32D STREET, SHOWING UNION DIME SAVINGS INSTITUTION.

TOMB OF GEN. U. S. GRANT, RIVERSIDE PARK, N. Y.

CENTRAL PARK ENTRANCE, AT SEVENTH AVENUE AND 59TH STREET.

F. A. O. SCHWARZ, 42 EAST 14TH STREET,
UNION SQUARE.

THE BOWERY, LOOKING NORTHWARD FROM GRAND STREET.

GRAND STREET, LOOKING EASTWARD FROM THE BOWERY.

MADISON SQUARE, SHOWING FIFTH-AVENUE, ALBEMARLE, HOFFMAN AND

FIFTH AVENUE AND BROADWAY, BETWEEN 23D AND 27TH STREETS.

MES HOTELS.

GENERAL THEOLOGICAL
CHELSEA SQUARE.

SEMINARY OF THE PROTESTANT EPISCOPAL CHURCH.

NINTH AND TENTH AVENUES, 20TH AND 21ST STREETS.

POTTIER, STYMUS & COMPANY.

LEXINGTON AVENUE, NORTHEAST CORNER 41ST STREET.

ST. FRANCIS XAVIER CHURCH AND COLLEGE, ROMAN CATHOLIC. 36 WEST 16TH STREET, BETWEEN FIFTH AND SIXTH AVENUES.

JAMES McCREERY & CO., BROADWAY, NORTHWEST CORNER OF 11TH STREET.

LORD & TAYLOR, BROADWAY, SOUTHWEST CORNER OF 20TH STREET.

MOUNT ST. VINCENT ACADEMY, RIVERDALE, BEYOND THE HARLEM RIVER.

ST. CATHERINE'S CONVENT, MADISON AVENUE AND EAST 81st STREET.

THE GORHAM MANUFACTURING COMPANY.
BROADWAY, NORTHWEST CORNER OF 19TH STREET.

THE BOWERY.
LOOKING NORTH FROM CANAL STREET.

PARLOR

MORTIMER BUILDING.

WALL STREET, SOUTH SIDE, CORNER OF NEW STREET.

FOURTH AVENUE AND MURRAY HILL HOTEL, FROM GRAND CENTRAL STATION.

INTERIOR OF DICKEL'S RIDING ACADEMY, 124 TO 138 WEST 56TH STREET.

JEFFERSON-MARKET POLICE COURT.

SIXTH AVENUE, WEST SIDE, FROM GREENWICH AVENUE TO 10TH STREET.

BENNETT BUILDING.

NASSAU, FULTON AND ANN STREETS.

DICKEL'S RIDING ACADEMY, 124 TO 136 WEST 56TH STREET.

METROPOLITAN MUSEUM OF ART.
CENTRAL PARK, NEAR FIFTH AVENUE AND 82D STREET.

INTERIOR OF THE METROPOLITAN MUSEUM OF ART.

POTTER BUILDING.
PARK ROW, NASSAU AND BEEKMAN STREETS.

AMERICAN MUSEUM OF NATURAL HISTORY.

CENTRAL PARK WEST, BETWEEN WEST 77TH AND WEST 81ST STREETS.

MILLS BUILDING.

BROAD STREET, WALL STREET AND EXCHANGE PLACE.

AMERICAN FINE-ARTS BUILDING, 215 WEST 57TH STREET.

BIRD'S-EYE VIEW OF FIFTH AVENUE.

NORTH OF 51ST STREET.

HEGGER'S ART ESTABLISHMENT, 152 BROADWAY, NEAR LIBERTY STREET.

FIFTH-AVENUE ART GALLERIES, 366 AND 368 FIFTH AVENUE.

WASHINGTON BUILDING.

BROADWAY, BATTERY PLACE AND BATTERY PARK.

TIFFANY GLASS AND DECORATING COMPANY, FOURTH AVENUE AND 25TH STREET.

RIVERSIDE DRIVE, CORNER OF 108TH STREET. RESIDENCE OF SAMUEL G. BAYNE.

THE BERWIND-WHITE COAL-MINING COMPANY.

COAL PIERS AND BARGES AT JERSEY CITY. OFFICES, 55 BROADWAY, NEW YORK.

AMERICAN INSTITUTE HALL, 1079 THIRD AVENUE, BETWEEN 63D AND 64TH STREETS.

LENOX LIBRARY, FIFTH AVENUE, 70TH AND 71ST STREETS.

STEINWAY & SONS.

PARK AVENUE, BETWEEN 52D AND 53D STREETS.

ASTOR LIBRARY, LAFAYETTE PLACE, BETWEEN ASTOR PLACE AND GREAT JONES STREET.

AMERICAN SUGAR-REFINING COMPANY.

THE HAVEMEYER AND BROOKLYN HOUSES. REFINERIES IN BROOKLYN. OFFICES, WALL AND SOUTH STREETS, NEW YORK.

FIFTH AVENUE, LOOKING NORTH FROM 42D STREET.

COLLEGIATE CHURCH, 5TH AVENUE AND WEST 48TH STREET.

TRINITY CHURCH -- PROTESTANT EPISCOPAL.

BROADWAY, BETWEEN RECTOR AND THAMES STREETS, AT THE HEAD OF WALL STREET.

COLLEGIATE REFORMED CHURCH, AT WEST-END AVENUE AND 77TH STREET.

ST. AUGUSTINE'S CHAPEL, PROTESTANT EPISCOPAL,
107 EAST HOUSTON STREET.

ST. PAUL'S CHAPEL--PROTESTANT EPISCOPAL.

BROADWAY AND CHURCH STREET, FROM FULTON STREET TO VESEY STREET.

CENTRAL STORES, TERMINAL WAREHOUSE COMPANY.

ELEVENTH AVENUE, NORTH RIVER, 27TH AND 28TH STREETS.

GRACE CHURCH — PROTESTANT EPISCOPAL.
BROADWAY, NEAR 10TH STREET, AT THE HEAD OF LOWER BROADWAY.

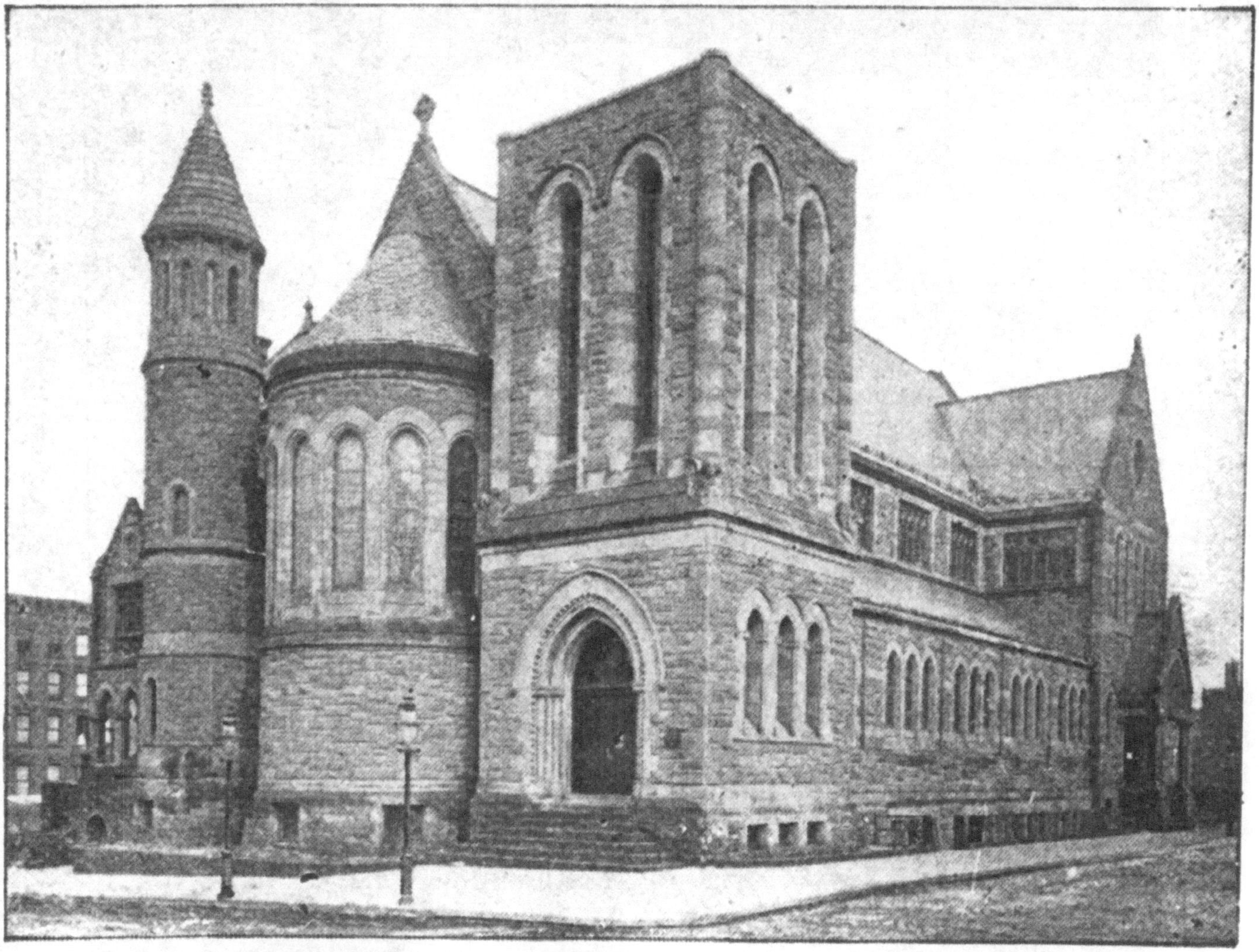

ST. JAMES'S CHURCH, PROTESTANT EPISCOPAL, MADISON AVENUE AND EAST 71ST STREET.

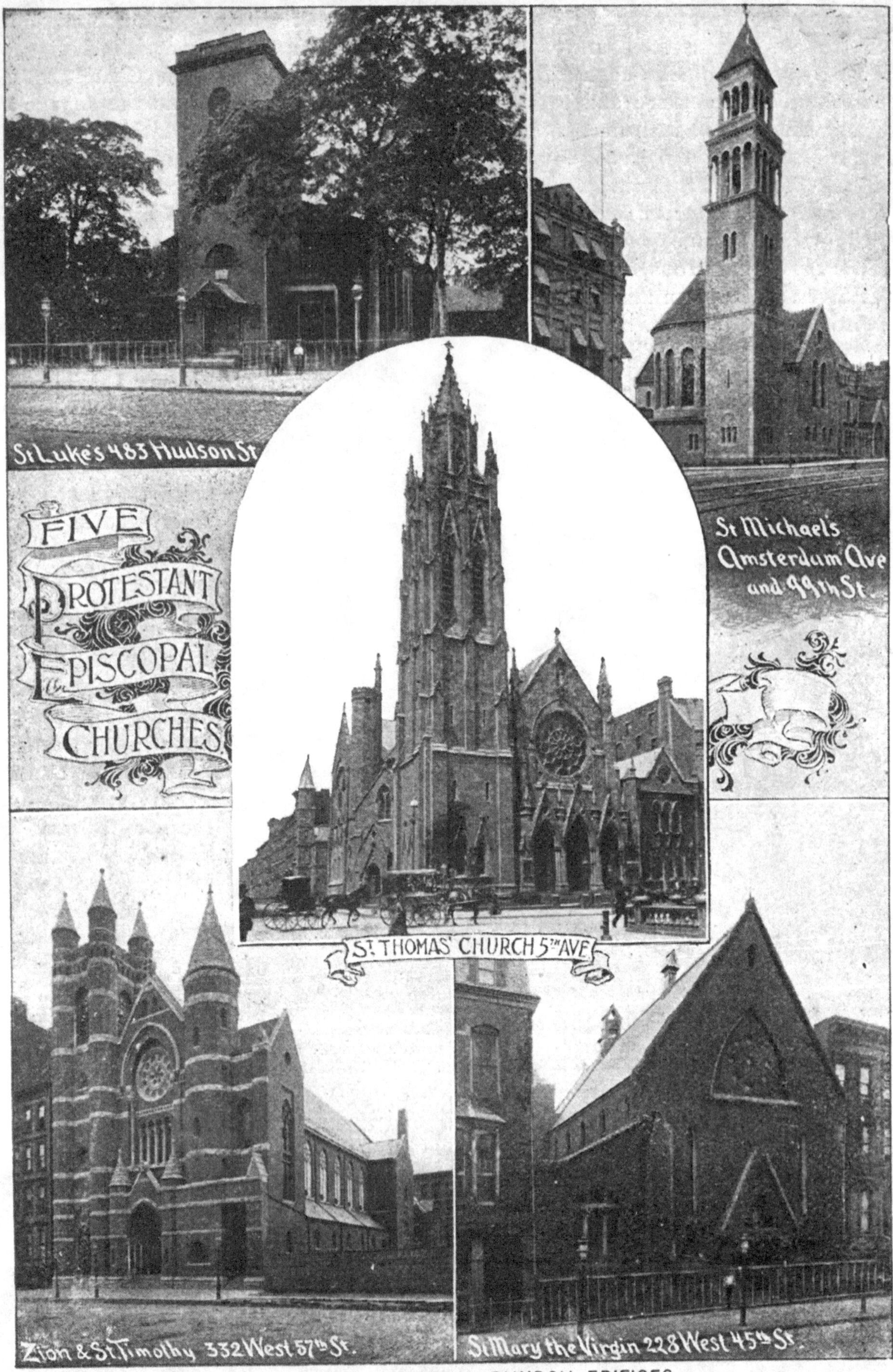

PROTESTANT EPISCOPAL CHURCH EDIFICES.

ST. LUKE'S. ST. MICHAEL'S. ST. THOMAS'. ZION AND ST. TIMOTHY. ST. MARY THE VIRGIN.

NEW-YORK CENTRAL & HUDSON-RIVER RAILROAD FREIGHT DEPOT ON HUDSON STREET.

CENTRE MARKET, GRAND AND CENTRE STREETS.

ST. BARTHOLOMEW'S CHURCH, PROTESTANT EPISCOPAL, MADISON AVENUE AND EAST 44TH STREET.

ALL SOULS' CHURCH, PROTESTANT EPISCOPAL, MADISON AVENUE AND EAST 66TH STREET.

ST. BARTHOLOMEW'S PARISH HOUSE, 205 EAST 42D STREET.

CHURCH OF THE HOLY TRINITY, PROTESTANT EPISCOPAL, MADISON AVENUE AND EAST 42D STREET.

CHURCH OF THE INCARNATION, PROTESTANT EPISCOPAL, MADISON AVENUE AND EAST 35TH STREET.

CATHEDRAL OF ST. JOHN THE DIVINE. (PROTESTANT EPISCOPAL.)

MORNINGSIDE PARK.

ST. PATRICK'S CATHEDRAL, ROMAN CATHOLIC.
FIFTH AVENUE, 50TH AND 51ST STREETS.

ST. PATRICK'S CATHEDRAL, ROMAN CATHOLIC.
THE HIGH ALTAR IN THE SANCTUARY, AT THE EASTERN END.

BETH ISRAEL BIKUR CHOLIM, HEBREW, LEXINGTON AVENUE AND EAST 72D STREET.

THE BIBLE HOUSE OF THE AMERICAN BIBLE SOCIETY.

THIRD AND FOURTH AVENUES, FROM 8TH TO 9TH STREETS, OPPOSITE ASTOR PLACE

THE PROVIDENT SAVINGS LIFE-ASSURANCE SOCIETY,
COLUMBIA BUILDING, BROADWAY AND MORRIS STREET.

NEW-YORK CITY ASYLUM FOR THE INSANE (WOMEN), BLACKWELL'S ISLAND.

NEW-YORK CITY ASYLUM FOR THE INSANE (MEN), WARD'S ISLAND.

FIFTH AVENUE ON A SUNDAY MORNING.

LOOKING NORTH FROM THE CATHEDRAL.

FOURTH-AVENUE PRESBYTERIAN CHURCH. ASSOCIATION HALL. 23D STREET.

YOUNG MEN'S CHRISTIAN ASSOCIATION, 23D STREET AND FOURTH AVENUE.

YOUNG MEN'S INSTITUTE, Y. M. C. A., 222 BOWERY.

NEW-YORK SOCIETY FOR THE RELIEF OF THE RUPTURED AND CRIPPLED, LEXINGTON AVENUE AND EAST 42D STREET.

MOUNT-SINAI HOSPITAL, LEXINGTON AVENUE, EAST 66TH AND 67TH STREETS.

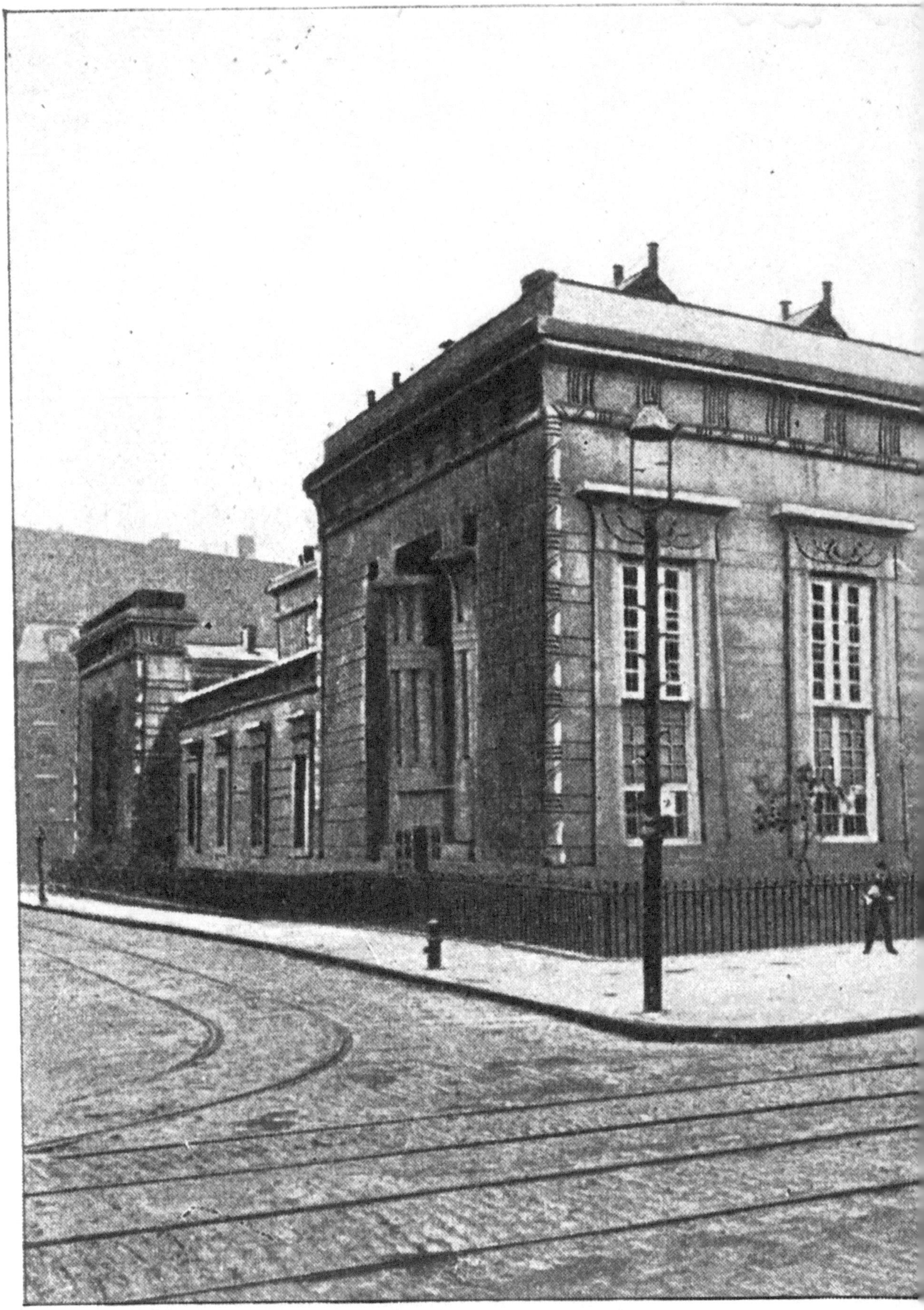

THE TOMBS. THE PLACE OF
FRANKLIN, CENTRE, LEONARD AND ELM STREETS.

DETENTION FOR CRIMINALS AWAITING TRIAL.

BLACKWELL'S ISLAND INSTITUTIONS.

THE CHARITY HOSPITAL, PENITENTIARY WORKSHOPS, AND CHURCHES.

SCENES ON BLACKWELL'S ISLAND.

THE ALMS-HOUSE CHAPEL, OLD BLACKWELL RESIDENCE, AND OTHER BUILDINGS.

SUSPENSION BRIDGE, TRINITY-CHURCH CEMETERY, ELEVENTH AVENUE AND 155TH STREET.

POLICE BOAT "PATROL," PIER A, NORTH RIVER.

TRINITY CHURCH.
BROADWAY, OPPOSITE WALL STREET.

KENSICO CEMETERY.

CEMETERY AT KENSICO STATION ON HARLEM RAILROAD. EAST 42D STREET, NEW YORK.

KENSICO CEMETERY
FROM NATIONAL GROUNDS.

TATION
EMETERY-

CASTLE WILLIAMS, GOVERNOR'S ISLAND.

EIGHTH REGIMENT ARMORY. PARK AVENUE, FROM 94TH TO 95TH STREET.

U.-S. LINE-OF-BATTLE SHIP "NEW HAMPSHIRE," HEADQUARTERS OF THE NAVAL BATTALION, EAST RIVER, AT THE FOOT OF EAST 28TH STREET.

FIRE-BOAT "NEW-YORKER," AT CASTLE-GARDEN BULKHEAD.

RIDING CLUB. DICKEL'S RIDING ACADEMY. TROOP A.

RIDING CLUB AND TROOP A ARMORY, 130 WEST 56TH STREET.

MASONIC TEMPLE, 23D STREET AND SIXTH AVENUE.

DEUTSCH-AMERIKANISCHE SCHUETZEN GESELLSCHAFT,
12 ST. MARK'S PLACE, NEAR THIRD AVENUE.

SCOTTISH RITE HALL, MADISON AVENUE AND 29TH STREET.

THE CRYSTAL PALACE OF 1853, IN BRYANT PARK.

RIDING CLUB, 58TH STREET, NORTH SIDE, BETWEEN FIFTH AND MADISON AVENUES.

CASTLE GARDEN, BATTERY PARK, AS IT IS.

MADISON-SQUARE GARDEN, FOURTH-AVENUE PORTICO AND 26TH-STREET FRONT.

MADISON-SQUARE GARDEN.

MADISON SQUARE, MADISON AND FOURTH AVENUES, AND WEST 26TH AND WEST 27TH STREETS.

CARNEGIE MUSIC HALL, SEVENTH AVENUE, SOUTHEAST CORNER OF 57TH STREET.

METROPOLITAN OPERA-HOUSE.

BROADWAY, SEVENTH AVENUE, 39TH AND 40TH STREETS.

PALMER'S THEATRE (AS IT IS), BROADWAY, NORTHEAST CORNER OF 30TH STREET.

BROADWAY AND 40TH STREET, SHOWING EMPIRE THEATRE AND ORIENTAL HOTEL.

EIGHTH AVENUE AND 42D STREET. SHOWING AMERICAN THEATRE.

HOYT'S MADISON-SQUARE THEATRE, 24TH STREET, NEAR BROADWAY.

PROCTOR'S THEATRE, 141 WEST 23D STREET, NEAR SIXTH AVENUE.

STEINWAY HALL, 109-111 EAST 14TH STREET, NEAR FOURTH AVENUE.

BROADWAY AND 28TH STREET, SHOWING FIFTH-AVENUE THEATRE, GILSEY BUILDING, AND HERRMANN'S THEATRE.

BROADWAY AND 39TH STREET, SHOWING CASINO THEATRE, ABBEY'S THEATRE, AND HOTEL NORMANDIE.

"THE EVENING POST" AND "THE NATION," EVENING POST BUILDING.
BROADWAY, SOUTHEAST CORNER OF FULTON STREET.

" THE SUN," NASSAU AND FRANKFORT STREETS.

"SUN." "DAY-BOOK." "TRIBUNE." "TIMES." "WORLD."

PRINTING-HOUSE SQUARE IN 1868.

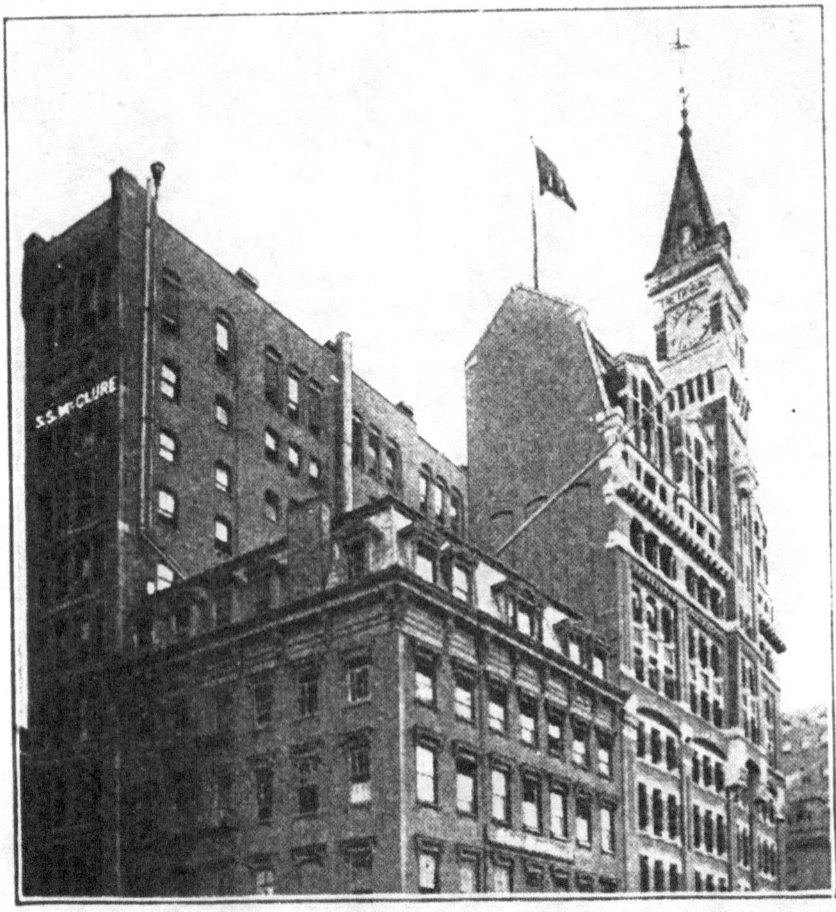

"THE SUN" AND "THE TRIBUNE."

THE "MAIL AND EXPRESS" BUILDING.

BROADWAY, SOUTHWEST CORNER OF FULTON STREET; OPPOSITE ST. PAUL'S CHURCHYARD.

FIFTH AVENUE, LOOKING NORTH FROM 40TH STREET.

BROADWAY, SIXTH AVENUE AND 35TH STREET, SHOWING "HERALD" BUILDING AND DODGE STATUE.

THE "WORLD" BUILDING -- PARK ROW AND FRANKFORT STREET.
AS SEEN FROM BROADWAY, ACROSS CITY-HALL PARK.

NASSAU STREET. "THE TIMES." PARK ROW.

THE "NEW-YORK TIMES" BUILDING-

PRINTING-HOUSE SQUARE, CIT

ROW, NASSAU AND SPRUCE STREETS.

PARK AND THE POST OFFICE.

"NEWS." "ADVERTISER."

PARK ROW, THE OLDER "NEWSPAPER ROW."

MAIL AND EXPRESS
THE MAIL AND EXPRESS
RECORDER.
New York
Recorde
MAIL & EXPRESS

NEW-YORK HERALD BUILDING, BROADWAY AND ANN STREET.

NEW-YORK HERALD BUILDING (IN CONSTRUCTION), BROADWAY AND 35TH STREET.

EPISCOPAL DIOCESAN HOUSE. COLONNADE ROW. "THE CHURCHMAN."

"THE CHURCHMAN," 47 LAFAYETTE PLACE, OPPOSITE ASTOR LIBRARY.

"CITY HALL." "WORLD." "SUN." "JOURNAL." "TRIBUNE."

CITY-HALL PARK, FROM BROADWAY TO PARK ROW.

THE DAILY PAPERS AND PROMINENT BUILDINGS OF "NEWSPAPER ROW."

POTTER BUILDING. "PRESS." TEMPLE COURT. POST OFFICE.

FRANKLIN SQUARE AND THE HARPERS' PUBLISHING HOUSE.

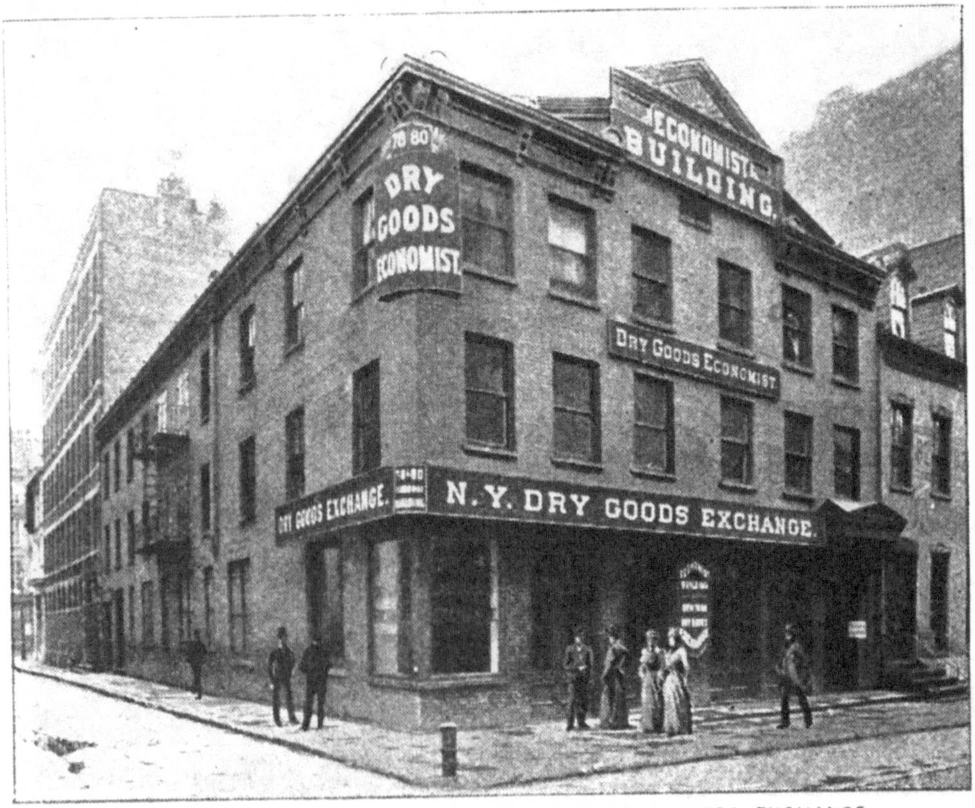

"DRY GOODS ECONOMIST" AND NEW-YORK DRY GOODS EXCHANGE,
78 AND 80 WALKER STREET.

"JUDGE" BUILDING, THE HOME OF FRANK LESLIE'S PUBLICATIONS, FIFTH AVENUE AND 16TH STREET.

COLUMBIA BUILDING. TRINITY CHURCH. BROADWAY. MANHATTAN LIFE BUILDING. CONSOLIDATED EXCHANGE. STANDARD OIL BUILDING

LOWER BROADWAY.

LOOKING NORTH FROM BOWLING GREEN.

PUCK BUILDING,

EAST HOUSTON AND MULBERRY STREETS.

NEW-YORK BOWERY FIRE-INSURANCE COMPANY, BOWERY AND GRAND STREET.

RUTGERS FIRE-INSURANCE CO., PARK ROW, WORTH AND MOTT STREETS.

CANAL, VESTRY, AND VARICK STREETS, SHOWING ST. JOHN'S CHURCH.

BROADWAY AND ASTOR PLACE, LOOKING SOUTHWARD ON BROADWAY.

MUTUAL FIRE-INSURANCE CO., 49 CEDAR STREET.

CUSTOM HOUSE. ATLANTIC MUTUAL.

WILLIAM STREET: LOOKING TOWARDS EXCHANGE PLACE FROM WALL STREET, AND SHOWING SITE FOR PROPOSED BUILDING OF NORTH BRITISH & MERCANTILE INSURANCE CO.

NEW-YORK LIFE-INSURANCE COMPANY.

346 AND 348 BROADWAY, SOUTHEAST CORNER OF LEONARD STREET.

MUTUAL LIFE-INSURANCE COMPANY OF NEW YORK.

NASSAU, LIBERTY AND CEDAR STREETS.

MUTUAL LIFE INS. CO.
KING'S HANDBOOK OF NEW YORK CITY

THE MANHATTAN LIFE-INSURANCE COMPANY OF NEW YORK.

64 AND 66 BROADWAY (NOW BUILDING), BETWEEN WALL STREET AND EXCHANGE PLACE.

THE EQUITABLE LIFE-ASSURANCE SOCIETY OF THE UNITED STATES.
BROADWAY, BETWEEN PINE AND CEDAR STREETS.

HOME LIFE-INSURANCE CO. OF NEW YORK.

BROADWAY, WEST SIDE, BETWEEN MURRAY AND WARREN STREETS, OPPOSITE CITY-HALL PARK.

PRODUCE EXCHANGE. BOWLING GREEN. STEAMSHIP ROW.

BROADWAY AT ITS BEGINNING.

METROPOLITAN LIFE-INSURANCE COMPANY.

METROPOLITAN LIFE BUILDING: MADISON SQUARE, 23D STREET AND MADISON AVENUE.

MUTUAL RESERVE FUND LIFE ASSOCIATION.

MUTUAL RESERVE BUILDING, BROADWAY, NORTHWEST CORNER OF DUANE STREET.

BIRD'S-EYE VIEW FROM THE WASHINGTON BUILDING.

LOOKING NORTHWEST.

AMERICAN
BANK NOTE CO.

WALL STREET, NORTH SIDE, NEAR WILLIAM STREET, IN 1860.

WALL STREET, FROM THE ASSAY OFFICE TO TRINITY CHURCH.

WALL STREET, SOUTH SIDE, FROM THE CUSTOM HOUSE TO BROAD STREET.

UNITED-STATES SUB-TREASURY, WALL AND NASSAU STREETS.

BANK OF NEW YORK, N. B. A., WALL AND WILLIAM STREETS.

GALLATIN BANK. THOMPSON BUILDING. MANHATTAN BANK. MERCHANTS' BANK. BANK OF AMERICA.

WALL STREET, NORTH SIDE, FROM WILLIAM TO NASSAU STREETS.

32 TO 46 WALL STREET.

ATLANTIC MUTUAL. UNITED STATES TRUST CO. UNITED STATES NATIONAL BANK. METROPOLITAN TRUST CO.

WALL STREET, SOUTH SIDE, FROM WILLIAM TO NASSAU STREETS.

37 TO 51 WALL STREET.

BANK OF AMERICA.

WALL STREET, NORTHWEST CORNER OF WILLIAM STREET.

NATIONAL CITY BANK OF NEW YORK.

52 WALL STREET, NORTH SIDE, BETWEEN PEARL AND WILLIAM STREETS.

NATIONAL BUTCHERS' AND DROVERS' BANK, BOWERY AND GRAND STREET.

THE NATIONAL PARK BANK OF NEW YORK.

214 BROADWAY, BETWEEN FULTON AND ANN STREETS, OPPOSITE ST. PAUL'S CHAPEL.

BROOKLYN BRIDGE, EAST FROM UNITED STATES ARMY BUILDING.

NORTHEAST FROM UNITED STATES ARMY BUILDING, SHOWING EAST RIVER AND BROOKLYN.

BATTERY PARK, ELEVATED RAILROADS AT SOUTH AND STATEN ISLAND FERRIES, AND BARGE OFFICE.

CASTLE GARDEN, FROM BATTERY PLACE.

TRINITY CHURCH. NEW-YORK LIFE-INSURANCE & TRUST CO.

NEW-YORK LIFE-INSURANCE & TRUST CO.

2 WALL STREET, NORTH SIDE, THREE DOORS EAST OF WILLIAM STREET.

MAITLAND, PHELPS & CO., EXCHANGE PLACE, BETWEEN WILLIAM AND HANOVER STREETS.

SKATING IN THE PARK.

NEW-YORK STOCK EXCHANGE.

BROAD, WALL AND NEW STREETS. INTERIOR OF THE MAIN FLOOR.

CUSTOM HOUSE, WALL STREET, HANOVER TO WILLIAM.

NEW-YORK STOCK EXCHANGE, BROAD STREET, NEAR WALL STREET.

NEW-YORK PRODUCE EXCHANGE.

WHITEHALL, BEAVER AND STONE STREETS, FRONTING BOWLING GREEN.

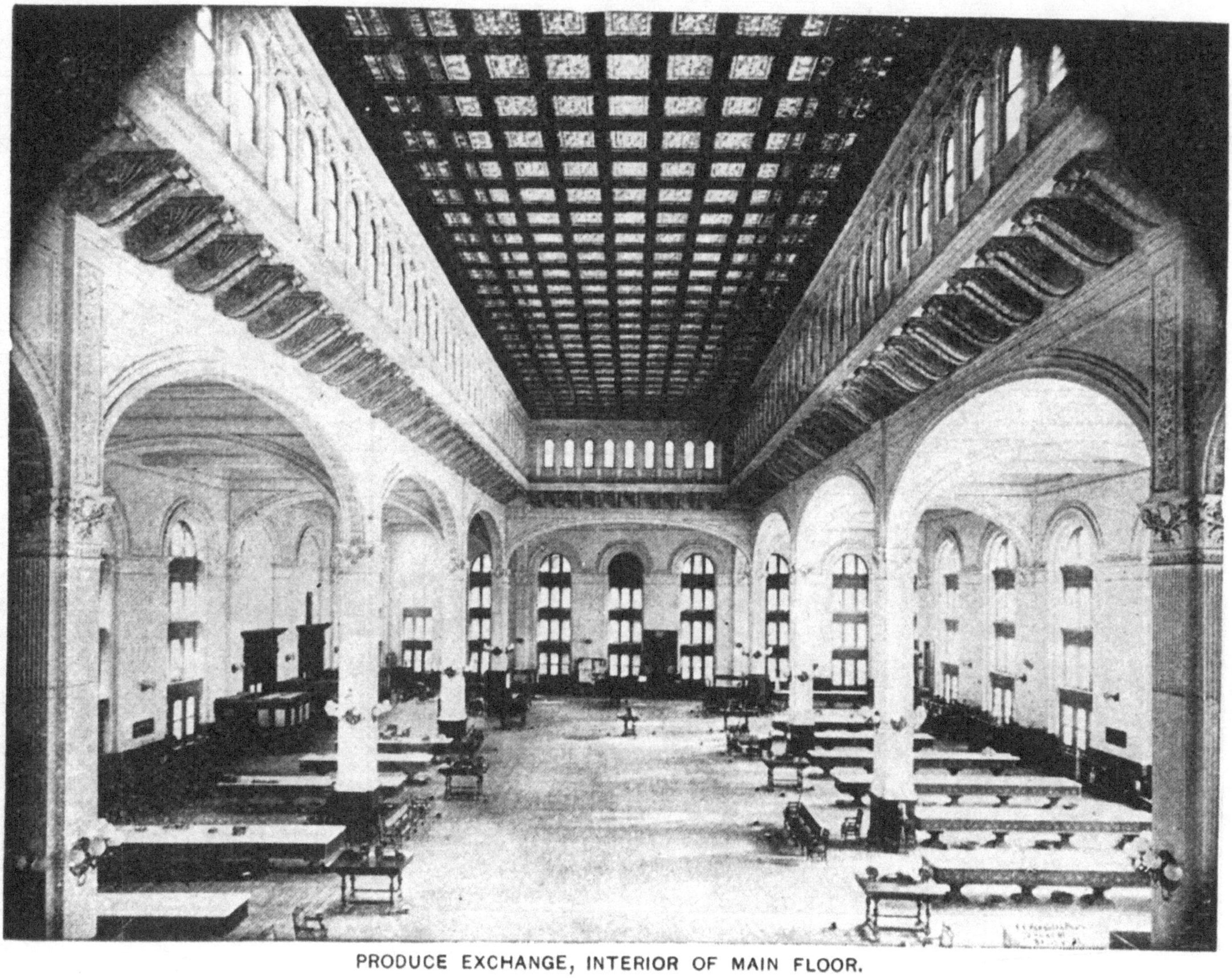

PRODUCE EXCHANGE, INTERIOR OF MAIN FLOOR.

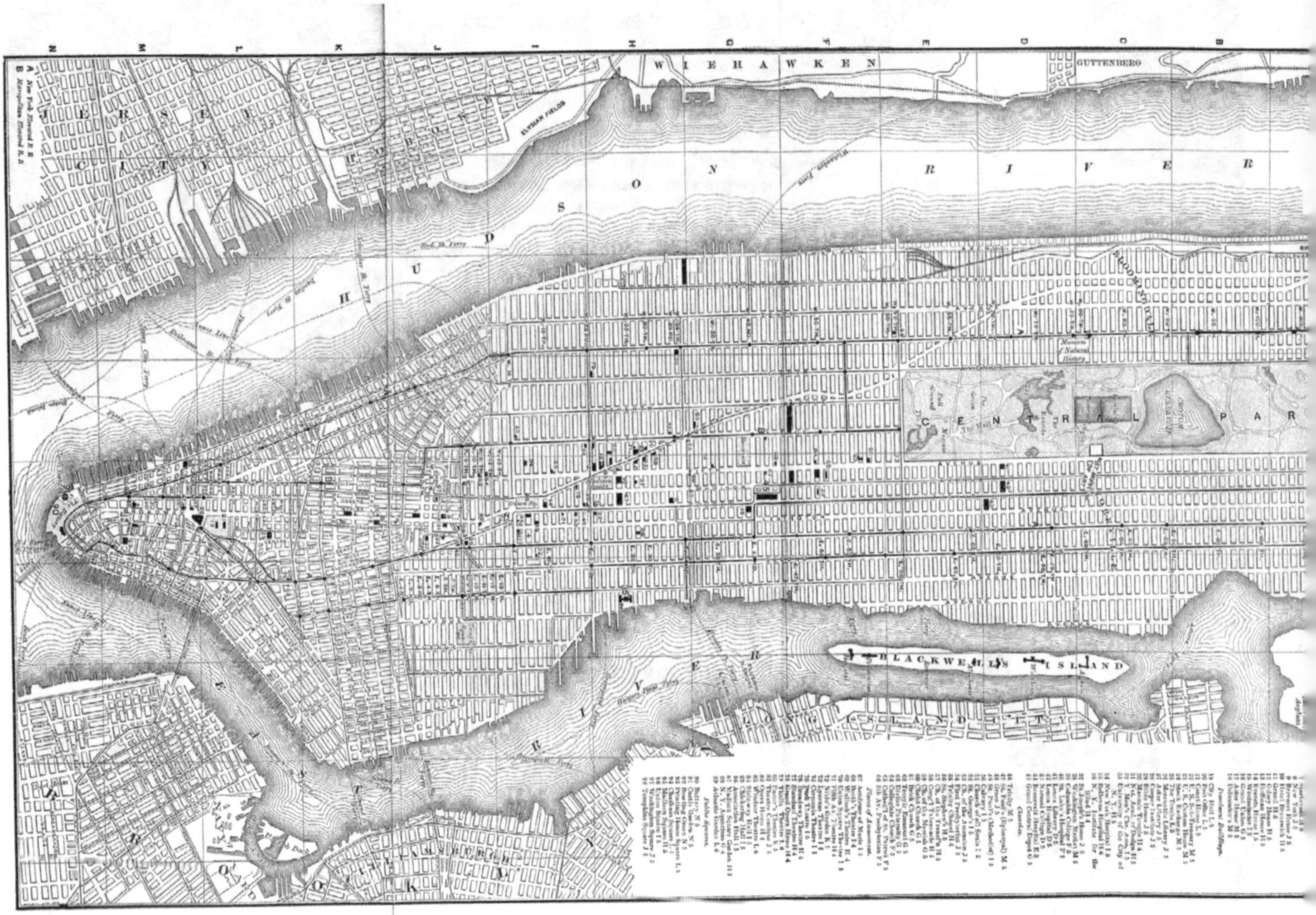
WIEHAWKEN
GUTTENBERG
ELYSIAN FIELDS
HOBOKEN
JERSEY CITY
HUDSON RIVER
CENTRAL PARK
Museum of Natural History
BLACKWELLS ISLAND
LONG ISLAND CITY
EAST RIVER
BROOKLYN

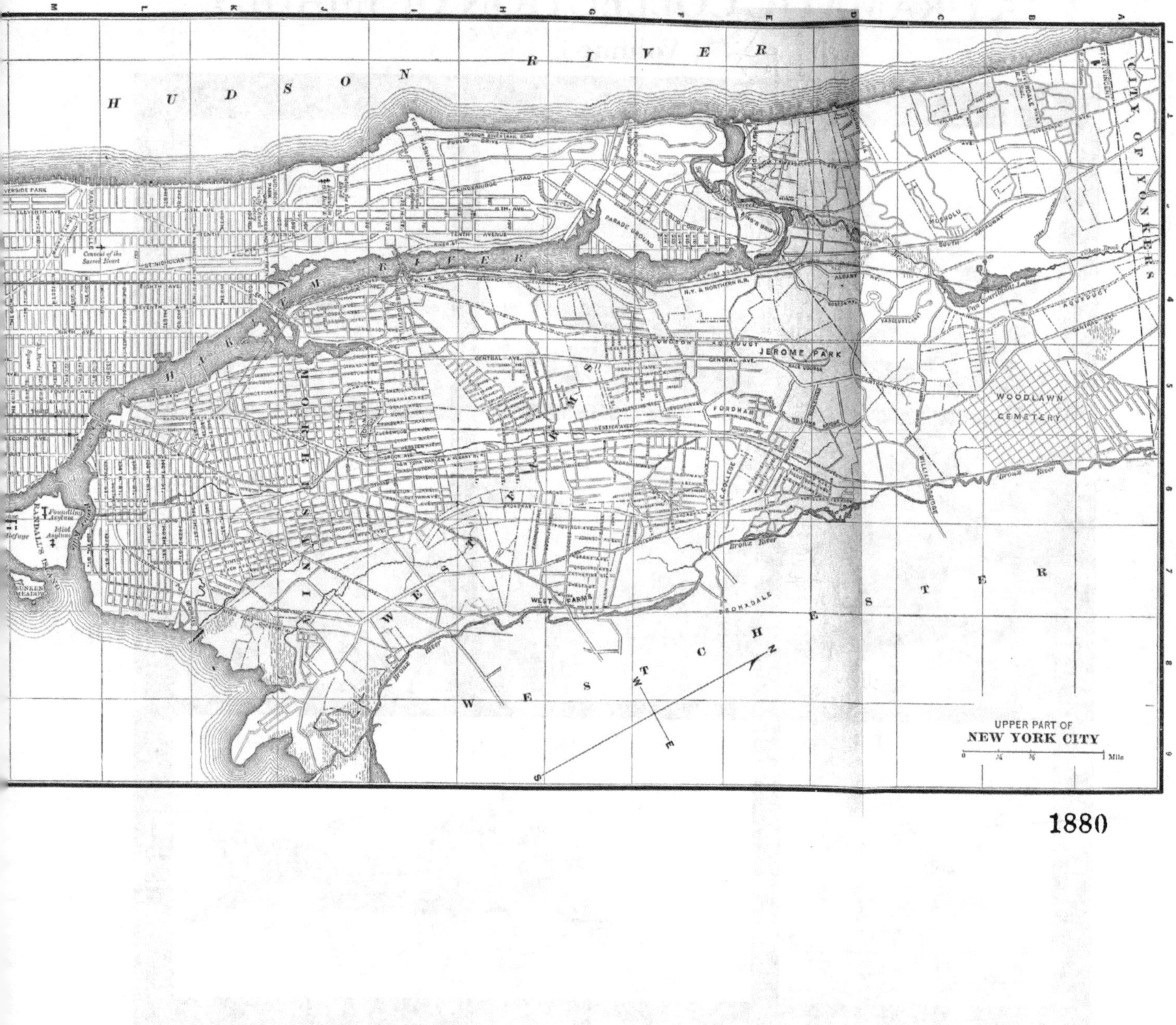
H U D S O N R I V E R
CITY OF YONKERS
JEROME PARK
WOODLAWN CEMETERY
FORDHAM
WEST FARMS
W E S T C H E S T E R
UPPER PART OF
NEW YORK CITY
Mile

1880

Also available from Classic Game Room Publishing:

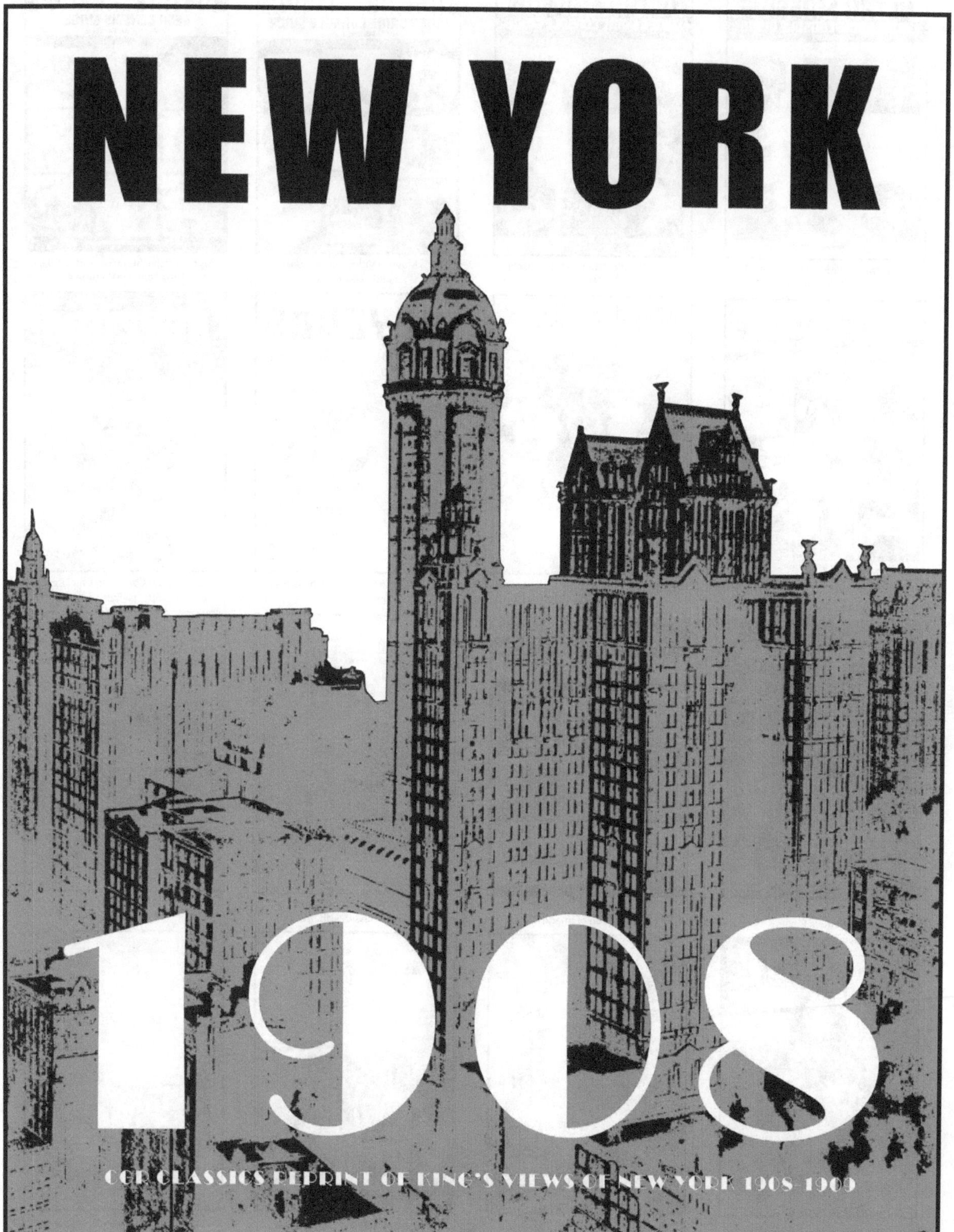

Other books from Classic Game Room Publishing at Amazon.com

Ultra Massive Video Game Console Guide Volume 1

Ultra Massive Video Game Console Guide Volume 2

Ultra Massive Video Game Console Guide Volume 3

Ultra Massive Sega Genesis Guide: Ultra Massive Volume 4

Ultra Massive Video Game Controller Guide Part 1: Ultra Massive 5

Retromegatrex Volume 1: The Lost Art of Mark Bussler 1995-2017

Heyzoos the Coked-Up Chicken #1 Special Edition

Heyzoos the Coked-Up Chicken #2 Special Edition

Pac-Man Collector's Guide: A Definitive Review

World War 1: A Dramatic Collection of Images

The Story of the Ship CGR Classics Edition

The White City of Color: 1893 World's Fair

Ethel the Cyborg Ninja Book 1

World's Fair of 1893 Ultra Massive Photographic Adventure

World's Fair of 1893 Ultra Massive Photographic Adventure 2

World's Fair of 1893 Ultra Massive Photographic Adventure 3

Other books from Classic Game Room Publishing at Amazon.com

Classic Game Room's Nintendo Switch Collector's Review Guide

How To Make A Video Game Review Show That Doesn't Suck

Video Game Tome of Infinity Volume 1

New York 1908 CGR Classics Edition

Lord Karnage 1.5 Special Edition

Kawaii Ocean: How to Draw Super Cute Sea Creatures Workbook

Official Guide to the World's Columbian Exposition

Why Nintendo Is Brilliant: NES Classic and SNES Classic Edition

The Great War Remastered WW1 Standard History Collection Vol. 1

The Great War Remastered WW1 Standard History Collection Vol. 7

The Great War Remastered WW1 Standard History Collection Vol. 12

The Great War Remastered WW1 Standard History Collection Vol. 14

Manga Teacup Cherry Blossom

Surf Panda #1

Old Timey Pictures With Silly Captions Volume 1

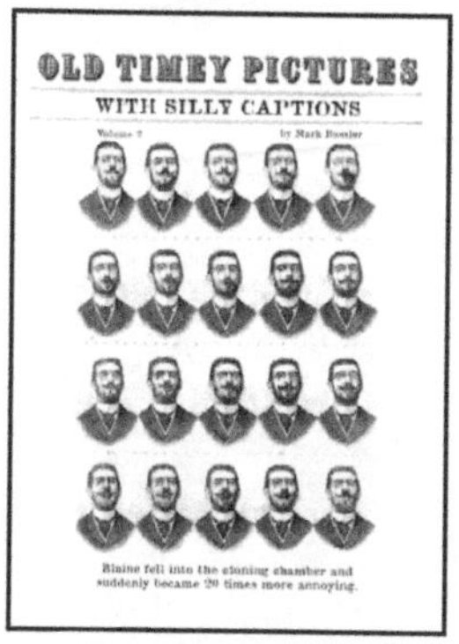

Old Timey Pictures With Silly Captions Volume 2

Follow Mark Bussler on Amazon for new book updates!

www.Amazon.com/author/MarkBussler

Subscribe to all my channels!

www.ClassicGameRoom.com
www.Amazon.com/v/ClassicGameRoom
www.Patreon.com/ClassicGameRoom
www.Instagram.com/ClassicGameRoom
www.Twitter.com/ClassicGameRoom

Mark's T-Shirts can be found on Amazon.com by searching
TURBO VOLCANO

New York in the 19th Century:
A Dramatic Collection of Images

Made in United States
Cleveland, OH
01 December 2024

11120546R00275